English Edition
英文注释

国文化入门

下册

《中国文化入门》编写组 编著

THRESHOLD OF CHINESE CULTURE
（VOLUME 2）

北京语言大学出版社
BEIJING LANGUAGE AND CULTURE UNIVERSITY PRESS

图书在版编目（CIP）数据

中国文化入门. 下/《中国文化入门》编写组编著
. -- 北京：北京语言大学出版社，2022.6（2024.9 重印）
ISBN 978-7-5619-6074-5

Ⅰ. ①中… Ⅱ. ①中… Ⅲ. ①中华文化－青少年读物
Ⅳ. ①K203-49

中国版本图书馆CIP数据核字(2022)第078700号

本书图片主要来自ChinaFotoPress汉华易美、壹图网、摄图网等网站。

中国文化入门（下）
ZHONGGUO WENHUA RUMEN（XIA）

策划编辑 上官雪娜
责任编辑 上官雪娜
英文翻译 李 菲 李 兴
英文编辑 侯晓娟
装帧设计 春天书装
责任印制 周 燚

出版发行 北京语言大学出版社
社　　址 北京市海淀区学院路15号，100083
网　　址 www.blcup.com
电子邮箱 service@blcup.com
电　　话 编 辑 部 8610-82303647/3592/3724
国内发行 8610-82303650/3591/3648
海外发行 8610-82303365/3080/3668
北语书店 8610-82303653
网购咨询 8610-82303908
印　　刷 北京富资园科技发展有限公司

版　　次 2022年12月第1版　　印　　次 2024年9月第2次印刷
开　　本 889毫米×1194毫米 1/16　　印　　张 13.25
字　　数 235千字
定　　价 98.00 元

PRINTED IN CHINA
凡有印装质量问题，本社负责调换。售后QQ1367565611，售后电话:010-82303590

导言

《中国文化入门》是一套为海外学习者设计的中国文化入门级通识型教学资源。如果你对中国文化抱有长久的兴趣，如果你已经具备一定的汉语知识和运用能力，如果你准备参加IB或AP的中文考试，这本通识型教材一定会让你受益匪浅！当然，作为一本文化教材，如果你的汉语基础还达不到要求，也不要放弃哦，本书为你准备了所有文字的英文翻译，帮助你摆脱语言困境。

《中国文化入门》由四个单元16课组成，每个单元名都是一个汉字，分别是“美、智、礼、和”。从第一单元“美”开始，到第四单元“和”结束，四个汉字带领你完成一趟由浅入深、由表及里的中国文化旅程，内容涉及地理山水、建筑设计、书画瓷器、文学音乐、衣食住行、古代科技、礼仪制度及儒释道思想等多个方面，包罗万象却并不艰涩难懂。若在这趟行程中，你对汉字、汉语或中国其他文化产生了更加浓厚的兴趣，我们将感到荣幸之至。当然，在深入阅读的过程中，我们也希望你能时时与自己国家或民族的文化做对比，看看它们与中国文化之间有什么相似点与不同点，在相互理解中求同存异，培养起全球化的视野与胸怀。

《中国文化入门》，称之为通识型教学资源，是因为它不仅是一套由上下册组成的印刷材料，还配有独立的在线学习小程序。在这个小程序上，你可以看到与本教材相关的教学课件、视频、动画、游戏、图集等教学资源。最值得你关注的，还有我们为该书专门摄制的学习微课。我们为每一课都配备了教师真人讲授的微课，时长为5–8分钟，包含每课所有知识点。它们不是教材的简单复制和背诵，而是对书上内容进行的提炼和补充，观看过程可以加深你对文化知识的二次理解。所以，在使用纸质资源之前，你可以先看一下微课，就像你平时刷YouTube的短视频一样，轻松地打开看看。也许从这里开始，你就喜欢上了这套学习资源。

最后，祝你拥有一趟完美的中国文化学习之旅！

编者

2022年10月

点击二维码，进入在线学习小程序。（2022年12月上线，敬请关注）

Preface

Threshold of Chinese Culture is a set of guiding interdisciplinary textbooks on Chinese culture for overseas learners. If you have a long lasting interest in Chinese culture, if you have certain knowledge about Chinese language and language proficiency certificates, or if you are ready to participate in the Chinese test of IB or AP, this set of interdisciplinary books will benefit you! Certainly, as a cultural textbook, if your Chinese proficiency is not up to the requirements, don't give up! This set of books provides you the translations of the whole content.

It consists of 16 lessons, divided into four units, and the title of each unit is one single character, respectively meaning "beauty", "wisdom", "etiquette", "harmony", beginning with the first unit "beauty", and ending with the fourth one "harmony". These characters lead us to a Chinese cultural journey which proceeds from the outside to the inside, including the geographical landscape, architectural designs, calligraphy, paintings, and porcelains, literature and music, livelihood, ancient science and technology, etiquette systems, and the fusion of Confucianism, Buddhism and Taoism, etc, all-inclusive but not hard to understand. We would be honoured if you've got a stronger interest in Chinese characters, Chinese language or other aspects of Chinese culture after learning it. Of course, in this thorough reading process, we also hope that you constantly compare Chinese culture with that of your own country or ethnic group, checking the similarities and differences between the two, seeking common ground while reserving differences in mutual understanding, and cultivating a globalized vision and mind.

This set of books is classified into the interdisciplinary teaching material, because it's not only a set of printing books consisting of two volumes, but also has an online mini program for further learning. Through this program, you could find a variety of media forms such as teaching coursewares, videos, cartoons, games and atlases about the books. What deserves your attention most is the micro-lectures we specially filmed for the books. There is a micro-lecture for each lesson in the books, lasting 5 to 8 minutes with all the knowledge points of it. This is not a simple copy and recitation of the books, but a refinement and supplement to the contents of the books. It can enhance your understanding of the cultural knowledge. So, before reading the books, you can watch the micro-lectures first, just like watching the short videos on YouTube. Maybe from it, you will enjoy this set of textbooks.

Lastly, wish you a perfect learning journey of Chinese culture!

The Authors

October 2022

Coming soon online in December 2022.

致　谢

《中国文化入门》的基本思路和主体内容来自于北京语言大学出版社2011年出版的多媒体数字产品《中国文化》。这个产品当时的几位作者是上官雪娜、周志宇、段宏江和高玉峰，向诸位表示感谢！此次将其作为教材改编，我们在文化教学需求调研基础上，对《中国文化》的结构和内容进行了完善和调整，修订和增补了大量内容，使之成为便于教学使用的文化教学资源，并将产品名字确定为《中国文化入门》。我们希望，借由《中国文化入门》，教师们有所凭恃，自然而畅达地带领学生展开精彩的中国文化之旅。此次编写的三位作者是上官雪娜、阮吕娜和刘晶，向三位老师表示感谢！

对于如何进行中国文化教学，如何进行文化教学产品的开发，除了诸位创作者付出的心血和努力，许多专家和同人也提出了宝贵的意见和建议。在此一并致以感谢！产品出版后，请各位继续关注，不吝灼见！

《中国文化入门》编写组

2022年6月

Acknowledgments

The basic idea and main contents of *Threshold of Chinese Culture* come from the multi-media digital product "Chinese Culture" published by BLCUP in 2011, the authors of which were Shangguan Xue'na, Zhou Zhiyu, Duan Hongjiang and Gao Yufeng, great gratitude to you all! Now, based on the investigation needs of cultural teaching, we have improved and adjusted the structure and contents of "Chinese Culture", adapting it into textbooks, revising and enriching large amounts of details, to make it convenient for cultural teaching, fixing the title *Threshold of Chinese Culture*. We hope that, depending on *Threshold of Chinese Culture*, teachers would take students to a wonderful journey of Chinese culture naturally and fluently. The three main authors of *Threshold of Chinese Culture* are Shangguan Xuena, Ruan lüna and Liu Jing, heartly thanks to the three scholars!

Apart from the painstaking efforts of the creators, many experts and colleagues have also put forward valuable opinions and suggestions on how to carry out Chinese culture teaching and how to develop cultural teaching products. We would like to express our appreciation to all. Please continue to pay attention to the textbooks and share your penetrating ideas!

The authoring group of *Threshold of Chinese Culture*
June, 2022

目　录
Contents

第三单元 Unit 3

第四单元 Unit 4

Unit 3
第三单元

礼 Etiquette

单元导入 | INTRODUCTION

中国人常用“礼仪之邦”来形容自己的国家，可见“礼”在中国非常重要。“礼”并不单纯指见面寒暄、握手问候，它渗透在衣食住行、待人接物，甚至国家管理等各个方面。几千年来，“礼”不断影响着中国人的言语和行为，所以，如果想深入中国人的内心，就需要了解与“礼”有关的文化现象。

Chinese people often use the phrase “the land of etiquette” to describe their country, from which we can see that etiquette is particularly important in China. Etiquette is not simply things like greetings and shaking hands, but permeates in every aspect, such as clothing, food, housing, transportation, treatment of people, and even national management. For thousands of years, it has constantly influenced the language and actions of Chinese people. Therefore, if you want to penetrate deeper into the hearts of Chinese, you must first understand the cultural phenomena related to etiquette.

09 百姓自以食为天

Food Is the Paramount Necessity of the People

热身 Warm-up

“民以食为天”，这是中国很有名的俗语。中国很早就进入了农业社会，大多数老百姓都从事农业生产。如果农业出了问题，皇帝就要着急，因为饿肚子的农民会反抗，他的“社稷”就可能保不住了。所谓社稷，其实就可以理解成国家，其中的“稷”是古代一种重要的粮食。我们不难从中看出饮食问题在中国文化中的重要性。

“Food is the paramount necessity of the people” is a famous Chinese saying. China became an agricultural society early, and the majority of its people work as farmers. If there were agricultural problems, the emperor was worried, as hungry farmers were apt to revolt, and it was possible he would lose control of his land. In ancient times, “earth and grain” was another word for “country”, from which we can see how important the issue of eating is in Chinese culture.

- 想一想，自己国家有哪些饮食习惯和餐桌礼仪？
  What are the eating habits and table manners in your country?

9.1 中国菜与烹饪

Chinese Food and Cooking

英文课文见P151

在漫长的农业文明发展过程中，中国人因地取材，逐渐形成了各地不同的饮食风俗。“南甜、北咸、东辣、西酸”是概括各地口味的一种说法。事实上，中国菜的种类极其丰富，即使你每天吃一道不同的菜，这一辈子也吃不完。中国有四大菜系和八大菜系的说法，一般来说，四大菜系指的是川菜①、鲁菜②、粤菜③和淮扬菜④。川菜排在第一，世界各地常见的“宫保鸡丁”“麻婆豆腐”等都属于川菜。由于许多华侨祖籍广东，粤菜在世界各地也比较常见。现在，中国菜的做法也在不断发生着变革，“东北菜”“湖南

菜”“上海菜”等各地菜品都独具特色。

如此丰富的中国菜，说到制作，最关键的是四个方面：选料、刀工、火候和调味。很多朋友爱吃的北京烤鸭，必须用北京地区的填鸭才行，这就是选料的问题；在烹饪前，做什么菜，原料就要相应地切成片、丝、条、块、丁、粒，而且必须均匀，才能保证良好的口感，这就是刀工；原料都准备好以后，不管你是炒、蒸、煮还是煎、炖、炸，火的大小和时间的长短可能就决定了菜肴的品质，这就是火候；调味则会影响到菜的风味，比如在川菜里辣椒是必不可少的，山西人做菜则离不开酸酸的醋。

注释 Notes

① 川：四川省的简称。
Chuan (川): It is short for Sichuan Province.

② 鲁：山东省的简称。
Lu (鲁) : It is short for Shandong Province.

③ 粤：广东省的简称。
Yue (粤): It is short for Guangdong Province.

④ 淮扬：江苏省扬州、淮安一带。
Huaiyang (淮扬) : It refers to the area of Yangzhou and Huaian, Jiangsu Province.

生词 Words and expressions

1	因地取材	yīndì-qǔcái	to obtain raw materials locally
2	风俗	fēngsú	custom; convention

3	华侨	huáqiáo	overseas Chinese
4	祖籍	zǔjí	ancestral home
5	变革	biàngé	to transform; to change
6	菜系	càixì	style of cooking
7	独具特色	dújù-tèsè	unique; peculiar
8	火候	huǒhou	duration and degree of heating, cooking, smelting, etc.
9	烹饪	pēngrèn	cooking
10	菜肴	càiyáo	cooked food (usually meat and fish dishes)

练习 Exercises

1 阅读课文，下列哪项不属于中国四大菜系？（　　）

Read the text and find out the one not among the four major cuisines in China.

A. 淮扬菜
- Huaiyang cuisine.

B. 粤菜
- Cantonese cuisine.

C. 鲁菜
- Shandong cuisine.

D. 上海菜
- Shanghai cuisine.

2 阅读课文，制作中国菜要关注哪些方面？［多选］（　　）

Read the text and find out what you need to pay attention to when making Chinese dishes. (Multiple Answer Question)

A. 调味
- Seasoning.

B. 火候
- Heat control.

C. 刀工
- Knife work.

D. 价格
- Price.

E. 选料

- The selection of materials.

3 阅读课文，关于中国菜，下面描述不正确的是哪一项？（　　）

Read the text and find out the wrong description on Chinese cuisine.

A. “宫保鸡丁”属于川菜

- “Kung pao chicken” belongs to Sichuan cuisine.

B. 原料被切成不同的形状会影响菜的口感

- Raw materials cut into different shapes will influence the taste of the dishes.

C. 不同地区的菜品有不同的风味

- Dishes in different regions have different flavors.

D. 最受外国人欢迎的菜系是粤菜

- Cantonese cuisine is the most popular cuisine among foreigners.

4 请辨别下列几种常见的中国菜的做法，并连线。

Identify the cooking methods of the following Chinese dishes and match the pictures.

A. 

B. 

C. 

蒸
Steam

炸
Deep-fry

煮
Boil

炒
Stir-fry

煎
Pan-fry

烤
Roast

D. 

E. 

F. 

5 请推荐一种自己国家的特色菜肴，并说说它的做法、口感和特点。

Recommend a special dish of your country, and tell us its cooking method, taste and characteristics.

9.2 餐桌与筷子

The Dining Table and Chopsticks

英文课文见P152

说了这么多中国菜，你也许会问这与“礼”有什么关系？事实上，中国古代的礼正是从饮食中诞生的。几千年前的人们通过饮食的差异来体现等级的不同，这种区分是极为严格的。今天，这些复杂的等级和规矩消失了，但与它有关的思想依然影响着今天的餐桌文化。

在美味的菜肴上桌以前，入座是一个重要的问题。职位高或年长的人坐在上座，上座一般指坐北朝南或正对着门的位置。入座的顺序，则一般是年长或饭局中比较重要的人先入座，其他人按职位或年龄长幼依次坐下，这叫作“尊卑有伦”[1]“长幼有序”[2]。

入座以后，吃饭也是有规矩的。这就不得不说到中国人独特的用餐工具——筷子。筷子是中国人发明的，后来东亚、东南亚各国受到中国影响，也以筷子为主要的用餐工具。看起来简单的筷子，具备的功能却非常多，两根筷子可以满足大部分进餐的需要。中国的

孩子很小就开始学习使用筷子。

在使用筷子吃饭时，需要注意的事情很多。比如，不能把筷子长短不齐地放在桌子上，这叫作“三长两短”，代表死亡，是不吉利的；不能用筷子敲打碗盘发出声音，因为民间认为，这样会变得像乞丐一样贫穷；筷子直直地插在饭碗里是绝对不允许的，因为这看起来就像祭祀时上香，很不吉利；另外，用筷子指人指物，把筷子放到嘴里咬住等，都是餐桌上比较忌讳的动作，是很失“礼”的行为。

注释 Notes

① 尊卑有伦：地位高和地位低的人之间有严格的顺序。

Zunbei Youlun: There is a strict order between people of high status and low status.

② 长幼有序：年长者和年少者之间是有顺序的。

Zhangyou Youxu: There is an order between the elder and the young.

生词 Words and expressions

1	体现	tǐxiàn	to embody; to reflect
2	规矩	guīju	rule; custom
3	职位	zhíwèi	occupation
4	入座	rùzuò	to have a seat
5	饭局	fànjú	dinner party
6	依次	yīcì	in sequence; one by one
7	吉利	jílì	lucky; auspicious
8	乞丐	qǐgài	beggar; pauper
9	忌讳	jìhuì	taboo

练习 Exercises

1 阅读课文，关于入座，下面描述不正确的是？（　　）

Read the text and find out the wrong description about seating in Chinese dining etiquette.

A. 一般年长的人先入座

- The elder people are usually seated first.

B. 职位高的人一般坐在坐北朝南的位置

- People with high position generally sit in a position facing south.

C. 一般按照职位高低和年龄长幼的顺序依次入座

- People are generally seated in the order of position and age, and the seniors are often seated first.

D. 上菜以后再依次入座

- After serving, you will be seated in turn.

2 阅读课文，下面哪些筷子的用法是不妥的？［多选］（　　）

Read the text and find out the inappropriate uses of chopsticks. (Multiple Answer Question)

A.

B.

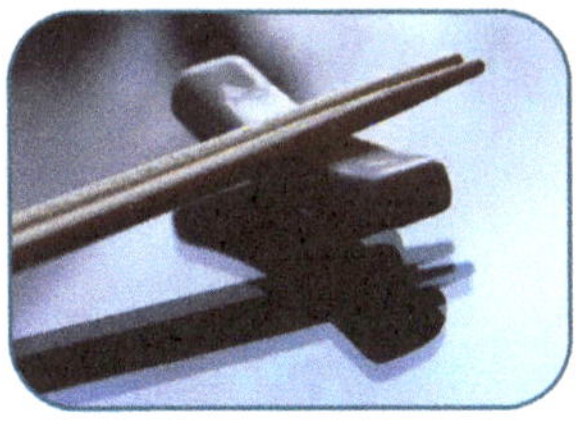

C.

D.

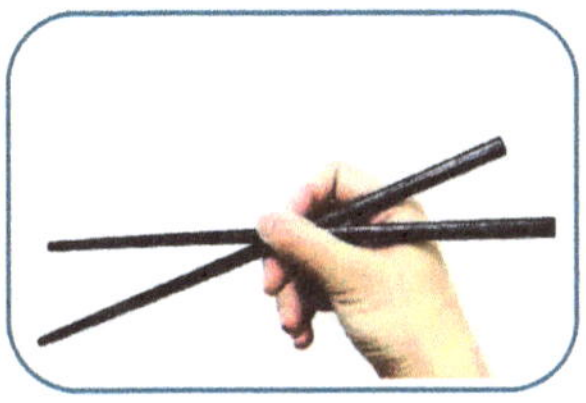

3 阅读课文，关于筷子，下面哪种描述是不正确的？（　　）

Read the text and find out the wrong description about chopsticks.

A. 中国孩子三四岁就会用筷子了

- Chinese kids can use chopsticks at the age of three or four.

B. 筷子起源于中国，后来传到东亚、东南亚其他国家

- Chopsticks are originated from China, and they then spread to other countries of East Asia and Southeast Asia.

C. 使用筷子有很多需要注意的礼仪

- There are a lot of etiquette to be aware of when using chopsticks.

D. 筷子是中国人唯一的用餐工具

- Chopsticks are the only dining tool for Chinese.

4 请介绍一下自己国家的餐桌礼仪，并说说它们与中国的餐桌礼仪有何异同。

Introduce the table manners in your country and talk about their differences and similarities with those in china.

9.3 酒席与酒礼

Banquet and Wine Ceremony

英文课文见P153

我们一直在说吃饭的事情，事实上，中国人说请人吃饭，可并不单纯指吃饭，特别是在正式的宴请中，酒是不可缺少的。所以中国人常说“无酒不成席”，并常常把宴请时用的餐桌称为酒桌或酒席。

中国自古以农业为主，所以绝大多数酒也是用粮食酿造的。中国酒主要有黄酒和白酒。黄酒是酿造酒，是中国独有的酒类。白酒是无色的蒸馏酒，它与法国白兰地①、俄罗斯伏特加②、苏格兰威士忌③并称为世界四大蒸馏酒。

在河南安阳出土的3000多年前的商代青铜器中，除了吃饭用的器皿，酒器也非常多。由此也可以看出，酒在中国的礼仪文化中的确扮演着很重要的角色。古代祭祀时，人们用酒来敬天地、敬先人，这种习俗一直流传到今天。文人创作时会借饮酒来获得灵感，唐代著名诗人李白就有“斗酒诗百篇”④的故事，意思是说他喝够了酒往往能写出好诗来。

醉饮图 明 万邦治

The Picture of Drunk Poets by Wan Bangzhi of Ming Dynasty

当然，酒最重要的功能是在酒桌上。客人入座后，主人要向客人敬酒，并且主人最好把一杯酒都喝光，这是一种礼，体现一种诚意；喝光以后，无论主人还是客人，都可以互相添酒，添酒必须要添满，这也是一种礼。就这样，在互相敬酒中，主客之间的交谈越来越深入，情感加深了，很多问题也在欢快的气氛中解决了。当然，如果你不会饮酒，最好事先说明，以免引起误解。

注释 Notes

① 白兰地：最初来自荷兰文Brandewijn，意为“烧制过的酒”，是一种高度蒸馏酒。
Brandy: It derives its name from the Dutch word Brandewijn, meaning “burned wine”. It is a kind of distilled liquor.

② 伏特加：俄罗斯的传统酒精饮料，是一种高度蒸馏酒。
Vodka: It is a traditional Russian alcoholic beverage, and it is a kind of highly distilled liquor.

③ 威士忌：是一种由大麦等谷物酿制而成的烈性蒸馏酒。
Whiskey: It is a kind of strong distilled liquor made from barley and other grains.

④ “斗酒诗百篇”：这句诗出自唐朝诗人杜甫的《饮中八仙歌》。斗（dǒu），中国古代计量单位，1斗约为2升。
“Composing a hundred poems after drinking two liters of liquor”: This line of poetry comes from *Extolling Eight Immortals in Drinking* by Du Fu, a poet of the Tang Dynasty. Dou, an ancient Chinese unit of measurement, is about 2 liters.

生词 Words and expressions

1	单纯	dānchún	purely; merely
2	正式	zhèngshì	formal
3	宴请	yànqǐng	dinner; banquet

4	酿造	niàngzào	to make (wine, vinegar, etc.); to brew (beer, etc.); to ferment
5	蒸馏	zhēngliú	to distill
6	器皿	qìmǐn	vessel
7	先人	xiānrén	ancestor; forefather
8	习俗	xísú	custom
9	灵感	línggǎn	inspiration
10	敬酒	jìngjiǔ	to propose a toast
11	诚意	chéngyì	sincerity
12	气氛	qìfēn	atmosphere
13	误解	wùjiě	to misunderstand

练习 Exercises

1 阅读课文，四张图片中哪张不是蒸馏酒？（　　）

Read the text and find out which of the following items is not distilled liquor.

A.

B.

C.

D.

2 阅读课文，从古至今的习俗文化中，酒扮演着哪些角色？［多选］（　　）

Read the text and find out the roles wine plays in the custom and culture that have been passed down from ancient times.

A. 文人借酒获得灵感

■ Literati get inspiration by drinking liquor.

B. 用酒祭祀天地和先人

■ Liquor is used to worship the heaven, the earth and ancestors.

C. 宴请中向客人表达诚意

■ It is used to express sincerity to the guests during the banquet.

D. 借酒消除忧愁

■ Some people eliminate sorrows by drinking liquor.

3 阅读课文，关于酒桌礼仪，下面哪个描述不正确？（　　）

Read the text and find out the wrong description about liquor in the table etiquette.

A. 主人要向客人敬酒，并把一杯酒喝光，代表诚意

■ The host should toast the guests and drink up a glass of liquor to show his sincerity.

B. 主人和客人互相添酒时要添满

■ When the host and the guest add liquor to each other's cup, they should fill it up.

C. 在互相敬酒中，随着主人和客人交谈的深入，情感也加深了

■ In toasting to each other, the host and the guest talk in depth and their relationship get a boost.

D. 在酒桌上为了表示诚意，一定要喝酒

■ In order to show sincerity at the table, people must drink.

4 思考题：想一想自己国家盛产什么酒？有哪些酒桌礼仪？

What kind of wine is your country famous for? What is the table etiquette on liquor?

9.4 茶与茶道

Tea and Tea Ceremony

英文课文见P154

茶与中国的丝绸、瓷器一样，在很多时候，是中国文化的符号。

中国人饮茶的历史与饮酒一样，非常漫长。1000多年前唐朝的陆羽写过一本《茶经》①，把饮茶的起源追溯到了4000年前。茶的品种非常丰富，统计起来有几千种，现在比较常见的类别有绿茶、红茶、乌龙茶。绿茶，不经过发酵，越新鲜越好，去杭州旅行时，很多人都会买的龙井，就是非常有名的绿茶；红茶是全发酵茶，比如中国的祁门红茶就很有名；乌龙茶是半发酵茶，也是中国很有特色的一种茶，安溪铁观音是乌龙茶中的名茶。花茶在中国人日常生活中也很常见，

它其实是在绿茶或红茶中加一些香花而制成的，喝起来有花的香味，比如最常见的茉莉花茶。

在中国古代，饮茶与吃饭、喝酒一样，也是一种讲“礼”的行为，称作“茶道”。饮茶的礼仪也影响了其他东亚国家，日本和韩国也都有各自的茶道。到了现代，古代复杂的茶道很多被简化了，但以茶为媒介的交际行为还很普遍。今天，待客时，主人一般都会给客人敬茶；多数饭店在招待客人时，也会先送上一杯茶。过去，如果要拜师学艺，在拜师仪式上一定要给师傅敬茶，师父接过茶杯喝一口，表示他同意收下这个徒弟。古代还有一种以茶会友的聚会，叫“茶会”，朋友们坐在一起鉴赏好茶，交流思想。到了现代，茶会变成了茶话会，大家坐在一起喝茶、聊天，变成了一种休闲娱乐的方式。另外，今天探望亲友，茶叶仍是常见的礼品。茶叶在中国人的生活中如此常见，所以俗话常说，老百姓生活中离不开的七样东西是——柴米油盐酱醋茶。

注释 Note

① 《茶经》：中国乃至世界上现存最早、最完整、最全面的一部介绍茶的专著，被誉为茶学百科全书，作者是唐代陆羽。

The Classic of Tea: It is the earliest, most complete and comprehensive monograph on tea in China and even in the world. It is known as the tea encyclopedia. The author of *The Classic of Tea* is Lu Yu of Tang Dynasty.

生词 Words and expressions

1	符号	fúhào	symbol; mark

2	起源	qǐyuán	origin
3	追溯	zhuīsù	trace back to
4	统计	tǒngjì	statistics
5	发酵	fājiào	fermentation
6	简化	jiǎnhuà	to simplify
7	媒介	méijiè	medium
8	拜师	bàishī	to formally acknowledge somebody as one's master
9	鉴赏	jiànshǎng	to appreciate
10	礼品	zèngpǐn	(complimentary) gift
11	俗话	súhuà	common saying; proverb

练习 Exercises

1 阅读第九课课文，判断下面的表达是否正确。

Read Lesson 9 and tell whether the following statements are true or false.

1）中国四大菜系包括川菜、鲁菜、粤菜和淮扬菜。（ ）

■ The four major Chinese cuisines are Sichuan cuisine, Shandong cuisine, Cantonese cuisine, and Huaiyang cuisine.

2）中国各地的风味概括来说是"南甜、北辣、东咸、西酸"。（ ）

■ The flavors of various parts of China are generally sweet in the south, spicy in the north, salty in the east, and sour in the west.

3）筷子是中国人主要的用餐工具，是由中国人发明的。（ ）

■ Chopsticks were invented by Chinese people and are the main dining tools for them.

4）职位高或年长的人坐在上座，一般是坐东朝西的位置。（　　）
- People with high positions or the seniors sit on the upper seat, usually in a position facing west.

5）客人入座后，要先主动向主人敬酒。（　　）
- After guests are seated, they should propose a toast to the host first.

6）比较常见的中国茶的类别有绿茶、红茶、茉莉花茶、乌龙茶等。（　　）
- The common types of Chinese tea are green tea, black tea, jasmine tea and oolong tea.

2 阅读课文，中国人饮茶的历史有多长？（　　）

Read the text and find out the length of Chinese people's tea drinking history according to the record.

A. 1000多年
- Over 1,000 years.

B. 4000多年
- Over 4,000 years.

C. 2000多年
- Over 2,000 years.

D. 3000多年
- Over 3,000 years.

3 阅读课文，将茶的品种与其相应的制作工艺及代表茶品连线。

Read the text and match the varieties of tea with their corresponding production techniques and representatives.

绿茶 Green tea	半发酵 Half-fermented	茉莉花茶 Jasmine tea
红茶 Black tea	不发酵 Unfermented	祁门红茶 Black tea from Qimen
乌龙茶 Oolong tea	绿茶或红茶中加入香花 Add fragrant flowers into green tea or black tea	安溪铁观音 Tieguanyin from Anxi County
花茶 Scented tea	完全发酵 Completely fermented	杭州龙井 Longjing tea in Hangzhou

4 阅读课文，俗话说老百姓生活中离不开的七样东西不包含下列哪项？（　　）

Read the text and find out which of the following is not included in the seven things people cannot live without.

A.

B.

C.

D.

5 思考题：想想自己国家的饮食文化有哪些特点，与中国的饮食文化相比有何异同？

Think about the characteristics of food culture in your country and the similarities and differences between it and Chinese food culture.

小结 Summary

“礼”字，最早的意思是用美酒敬拜神灵。华夏先人们尊重粮食，感恩神灵和祖先，并由此逐渐演化出一套完整的礼乐文化。与粮食息息相关，与土地密不可分，务实的中国人对生活的态度积极而投入，至今如此。

The character “*li* (礼)” originally meant to worship gods with good wine. Chinese ancestors paid their respect to food, and their gratitude to the gods and their ancestors. It gradually evolved into a set of ritual culture. Closely related to food and inseparable from land, pragmatic Chinese people have a positive and devoted attitude towards life, and remain so even today.

10

婚丧亲疏各有别

The Various Kinships and Etiquette of Marriages, Funerals, and Rituals

热身 Warm-up

婚事和丧事在中国也被称为红白喜事。红事指与婚礼有关的事，白事指与葬礼有关的事。一个称红事，一个称白事，这与人们在婚礼和丧礼时所穿的衣服和场景布置有关。在中国传统的颜色寓意中，红色一般代表喜庆和热烈，白色一般代表悲伤和不祥，这一点与西方国家有很大的不同。中国是个多民族的国家，各个民族的婚丧礼仪各有特色，但其中许多习俗是相似的。

Weddings and funerals in Chinese are together called “red and white occasions”, with red referring to weddings and white to funerals. This term is related to the clothes people wear and the decoration on such occasions. Unlike in the West, the color red traditionally implies joy and warmth, while white means sadness and misfortune. China is a country with many ethnic groups, each having its own etiquette for weddings and funerals, but there are some things they all have in common.

- 想一想，自己国家或民族的婚丧习俗有什么特点？其中有什么寓意和禁忌吗？
  What are the characteristics of wedding and funeral customs in your country or ethnic group? What color implications or taboos do it have?

10.1 婚姻与婚礼

Marriages and the Etiquette of Weddings

英文课文见P155

在中国的传统习俗中，婚礼是一个家庭非常重要的事情。家里有人结婚，一家人会把全部精力都集中在婚礼上。到了现代，大多数中国家庭依然重视婚礼，只是仪式变得简单了。

虽然婚礼的仪式简化了，但中国人仍然保留着很多传统的婚姻观念。古代中国人讲究门当户对，先由媒人把两家的情况介绍给对方，再由双方父母来确认婚事。所以，古代大多是包办婚姻，男女双方自己没有决定权。现代社会以自由恋爱为主，但门当户对的思想依然存

在。人们大多会挑选和自己家庭地位、经济实力和生活背景相似的人作为结婚对象。

中国传统婚礼都要挑日子，也就是挑所谓的黄道吉日[①]。这种习俗在民间依然存在，只是不再像古人那么严格，大多数时候是一种心理安慰，比如挑选含有数字8或6的日子。8，发音与发财的“发”相近，代表财富；6，代表顺利，比如中国人常说六六大顺。

婚礼当天，男方称为新郎，女方称为新娘。新郎要去新娘家“迎娶”。古代接新娘都用花轿，今天则换成了长长的花车队伍。传统婚礼中，新郎把新娘接回家后，就要进行“拜堂”[②]仪式，拜过堂才能正式成为夫妻。现代婚礼虽然没有拜堂的说法，但男女双方也会向两家的父母鞠躬，对他们的养育表示感恩。

中国有些民族在婚礼中还有独特的习俗，比如阿昌族的抢亲[③]、羌族的“逗新郎”[④]、壮族的抛绣球[⑤]等等。由于中国是个多民族的国家，经过几千年的融合，很多婚礼习俗相互借鉴，不同民族的婚庆礼仪都是中国文化的一部分。

注释 Notes

① 黄道吉日：黄道是指地球绕太阳公转的轨道平面与古人想象中的天球相交的大圆。旧时迷信星命之说，在黄道特定的几个时间点上，做事会顺利，称为“黄道吉日”。现在泛指吉利日子。

Ecliptic auspicious days: The ecliptic refers to the great circle where the earth's orbit around the sun intersects the celestial sphere in ancient Chinese people's imagination. In ancient times, ecliptic auspicious days refer to the several points in time in the ecliptic during which everything is suitable. Now it generally refers to auspicious days.

② 拜堂：汉族的婚礼习俗。在举行婚礼时，新郎新娘拜天地、拜父母，最后夫妻对拜，完成整个仪式。

Baitang (拜堂): It is a marriage custom of Han ethnic group. During the wedding ceremony, the bride and bridegroom bow to the heaven and the earth, bow to their parents, and finally they bow to each other.

③ 阿昌族的抢亲：阿昌族是中国人口较少的七个少数民族之一，仅生活在云南省。抢亲是阿昌族人缔结婚姻的一种古老方式，是指未婚男子将喜欢的未婚女子抢到自己家结婚成亲的习俗。

Kidnapping the bride in Achang ethnic group: Achang ethnic group is one of the seven ethnic minorities with a small population in China and its people only live in Yunnan Province. Kidnapping the bride is an ancient way for Achang ethnic group to enter into marriage. It refers to the custom of unmarried men snatching their favorite unmarried women into their own homes to get married.

④ 羌族的"逗新郎"：羌族是中国的少数民族之一，主要生活在四川省。羌族结婚操办喜事，新郎要陪新娘回娘家，在娘家的宴席上，娘家人给新郎用四尺长的筷子，筷子头上还用几个土豆坠着，新郎要用这种筷子，隔着几盏油灯去夹用肉丁和豆粒做成的菜，如果夹不起菜，或油灯烧着下巴，就要被罚酒。这种习俗称为"逗新郎"。

Teasing the bridegroom in Qiang ethnic group: Qiang ethnic group, one of China's ethnic minorities, is mainly distributed in Sichuan Province. For Qiang ethnic group's wedding ceremony, the bridegroom must accompany the bride back to her family. At the banquet in the bride's family, the bridegroom is provided with a pair of four-foot-long chopsticks, on which a few potatoes are pendent. The bridegroom should use this pair of chopsticks to pick up food made of diced meat and beans through lighted oil lamps. The bridegroom will be fined with liquor if he cannot pick up the food, or if the oil lamps burn his chin. Such a custom is called "teasing the bridegroom".

⑤ 壮族的抛绣球：壮族是中国人口最多的一个少数民族，主要生活在广西壮族自治区。抛绣球是当地男女青年传达情感的方式。一个姑娘若喜欢上一个男青年，可以将绣球有意抛给他，男方接过绣球，则表示也有意愿交往，可以把礼物系到绣球上回投给姑娘。

Throwing an embroidered ball in Zhuang ethnic group: Zhuang ethnic group, the most populous ethnic minority in China, is mainly distributed in Guangxi Zhuang Autonomous Region. Throwing an embroidered ball is a way for local young men and women to express their affections. If a girl likes a young man, she can throw an embroidered ball intentionally to him, and if the man also takes a fancy to the girl, he will accept the ball and add a gift on it before throwing it back.

生词 Words and expressions

1	观念	guānniàn	concept; perception
2	门当户对	méndāng-hùduì	well-matched marriage
3	媒人	méiren	matchmaker
4	包办	bāobàn	to take everything on oneself
5	迎娶	yíngqǔ	to marry (a woman)
6	花轿	huājiào	bridal sedan chair
7	鞠躬	jūgōng	to bow
8	感恩	gǎn'ēn	to feel grateful; to be thankful
9	借鉴	jièjiàn	to use for reference

练习 Exercises

1 阅读课文，下面哪项不是中国传统的婚姻观念？（　　）

Read the text and find out which of the following description does not conform to traditional Chinese ideas on marriage.

A. 父母决定儿女的婚事

- Parents make the decision in the marriage of their children.

B. 男女双方讲究门当户对
- Both men and women want to be properly matched.

C. 婚礼日期会挑选黄道吉日
- An auspicious day will be chosen for the wedding.

D. 男女双方自由恋爱
- Both men and women are free to arrange their own marriage.

2 阅读课文，在中国数字“6”有何含义？（　　）

Read the text and find out the implied meaning of the number “6” in China.

A. 发财
- Getting rich.

B. 长久
- Forever.

C. 顺利
- Being smooth.

D. 快乐
- Happiness.

3 查阅资料，中国人的婚礼上可以见到以下哪种剪纸图案？（　　）

Search the information and find out the paper-cut pattern generally seen on Chinese weddings.

A.

B.

C.

D.

4 阅读课文，辨别图片中的婚俗，并将其与对应的民族连线。
Read the text and identify the wedding customs in the pictures and match them with the corresponding ethnic groups.

A. 

B. 

C. 

D. 

壮族
Zhuang ethnic group

羌族
Qiang ethnic group

阿昌族
Achang ethnic group

汉族
Han ethnic group

10.2 丧葬与祭奠
The Etiquette of Funerals and Sacrifice

英文课文见P156

中国人很忌讳说“死”，或者跟“死”发音相同的字，比如“四”。为避讳说“死”字，人们会说“去世”“离世”或更庄重的“逝世”，认为人死后是离开现在生活的世界（阳间），到另一个世界（阴间）去了，因此也有“阳寿”①和“阴寿”②的说法。因为把人的死亡看成是到另一个世界生活，所以在中国古代，不管是有钱人家还是贫穷的人家，都或多或少会在坟墓里放一些死者生前的物品做陪葬。墓葬考古发现的大量陪葬品，为我们留下许多古人生活的痕迹。

中国人的丧事是非常肃穆和庄严的。中国传统的丧葬方式有很多种，比如土葬③、火葬④、天葬⑤、水葬⑥等，其中最常见的是土葬，成语“入土为安”指的就是土葬。

事实上，古代中国人在活着的时候就开始准备与葬礼有关的事情了。人们会关心坟墓的位置，并认为位置好的墓地会给后代带来好运，而不好的位置则会带来噩运。其次，家人还会给老人提前选好棺材，即使家庭比较贫穷，也首先要保证有一副棺材。亲人去世后，家人会为逝者穿上寿衣，放进棺材，在家里最重要的位置布置灵堂，并在逝者身边守三天三夜，这称为守灵。三天后可以“出殡”，家人们把棺材移放到墓地里。出殡时，亲人们会烧很多纸钱、纸房子、纸做的牛羊等，希望逝者在阴间同样能很好地生活。

中国有个传统节日清明节，一般在每年的4月5日左右。在清明节，人们会去探望逝者，到逝者坟前扫墓。人们为坟上添些新土，拔去长在上面的杂草，将各种食物、酒水摆好，烧上一炷香，然后叩头、行礼、祭拜。有些人家也会把祖先的牌位供奉在屋里进行祭拜。扫墓这种习俗已经有2500多年的历史了。现在，为了节约土地资源，中国很多地方已不实行土葬，扫墓也就渐渐变成了一种怀念故人的仪式。

注释 Notes

① 阳寿：指人活在人世的寿命。

Yangshou: It refers to the life span of a person in the world.

② 阴寿：迷信说法，指人死后到了阴间的寿命。

Yinshou: It refers to the life span of a person to the underworld after death according to superstition.

③ 土葬：一般是把人的遗体先装在棺材里，然后再把棺材埋在土中。

Burial in the earth: The body of the deceased is usually put in a coffin first, and then the coffin is buried in the soil.

④ 火葬：用火把遗体烧成骨灰，然后将骨灰安置在骨灰盒里，再埋入土中，或撒入水中、空中。

Cremation: The body of the deceased is burned into ashes with fire, and then placed in an urn and buried in the soil, or sprinkled in water or in the air.

⑤ 天葬：人死后将遗体运到指定地点，让秃鹫（或其他鸟类、兽类等）吞食。

Celestial burial: The body of the deceased is transported to a designated place for vultures (or other birds, beasts, etc.) to swallow.

⑥ 水葬：将死者遗体投于江河湖海。

Water burial: It is the burial method of throwing the body of the deceased into rivers, lakes and seas.

生词 Words and expressions

1	避讳	bìhuì	taboo

2	坟墓	fénmù	grave; tomb
3	陪葬	péizàng	to be buried with the dead
4	痕迹	hénjì	trace; trail
5	肃穆	sùmù	solemn and respectful
6	庄严	zhuāngyán	solemn; dignified
7	丧葬	sāngzàng	burial; funeral
8	入土为安	rùtǔwéi’ān	Burial brings peace to the deceased.
9	噩运	èyùn	bad luck
10	棺材	guāncai	coffin
11	逝者	shìzhě	the dead
12	寿衣	shòuyī	graveclothes; shroud
13	灵堂	língtáng	mourning hall
14	出殡	chūbìn	to carry a coffin to the cemetery
15	探望	tànwàng	to visit; to call on
16	炷	zhù	*a measure word for incense*
17	叩头	kòutóu	to kowtow
18	祭拜	jìbài	to worship
19	牌位	páiwèi	memorial tablet
20	供奉	gòngfèng	to enshrine and worship
21	资源	zīyuán	resource

练习 Exercises

1 阅读课文，下面哪种不是中国传统的丧葬方式？（　　）

Read the text and find out the one that is not a traditional Chinese funeral custom.

A. 天葬
- Celestial burial

B. 树葬
- Tree burial.

C. 水葬
- Water burial.

D. 火葬
- Cremation.

2 阅读课文，关于古代的丧葬仪式，以下哪种描述是不正确的？（　　）

Read the text and find out the wrong description about the ancient funeral rituals.

A. 会在坟墓里放一些死者生前的物品做陪葬
- They will bury with the deceased his items in the grave.

B. 从古代到现在，土葬依然是最常见的丧葬方式
- Burial in the earth is still the most common way of burial since ancient times.

C. 古人至少去世三天后才可以出殡
- Acient people held a funeral at least three days after death.

D. 古人认为墓地的位置会影响后代的运气
- Ancient people thought the location of a cemetery will affect the luck of later generations.

3 阅读课文，下面哪个是祭拜祖先的传统节日？（　　）

Read the text and find out the traditional festival for worshiping ancestors.

A. 清明节
- Tomb-Sweeping Day.

B. 中秋节
- Mid-Autumn Festival.

C. 端午节
- Dragon Boat Festival.

D. 元宵节
- Lantern Festival.

4 思考题：想一想在自己的国家人们是如何看待死亡的？有哪些禁忌？

How do people view death in your country? What are the taboos?

10.3 称谓与亲疏

Kinship Terminology and Relationships

英文课文见P157

如果与中国人生活在一起，懂得了基本的规范和禁忌，只能算过了第一关，日常生活中还有很多需要了解的文化细节，其中最需要熟悉的就是称谓。

姑姑、叔叔、姨、舅舅、侄子、外甥……即使在中国，由于现代家庭结构的简化，年轻一代也经常混淆称谓。但是，中国称谓受到传统思想和道德观念的影响，是礼节中非常重要的内容，也是一个人血缘、身份、地位的标志。因此，了解中国人的称谓文化，能使你更好地与中国人进行交流。

中国的亲属关系跟婚姻和血缘密切相关，可以分为宗亲、外亲、妻亲三类，对三类亲戚的称呼各不相同。

宗亲	以父亲的血缘为纽带的男性分支
外亲	以母亲的血缘为纽带的亲属

妻亲	与妻子有关的亲属

在称呼长辈时，爸爸的父亲叫爷爷，爸爸的母亲叫奶奶，爸爸的姐妹叫姑姑，爸爸的哥哥叫伯父，爸爸的弟弟叫叔叔；妈妈的父亲叫姥爷（外公），妈妈的母亲叫姥姥（外婆），妈妈的姐妹叫姨，妈妈的兄弟叫舅舅。在称呼平辈时，爸爸兄弟家的孩子是“堂”亲，比如堂姐、堂弟；爸爸姐妹家的孩子是“表”亲，妈妈家亲戚的孩子也是“表”亲，都称为表哥、表妹。在称呼晚辈时，如果是你兄弟们的后代，称为“侄子”或“侄女”；如果是你姐妹们的后代，则称为“外甥”或“外甥女”。

另外，夫妻双方父母的称呼也并不相同。丈夫对外人称呼妻子的父母为“岳父”（或丈人）和“岳母”（或丈母娘）；妻子对外人称呼丈夫的父母为“公公”和“婆婆”。但当着老人的面，则跟自己的

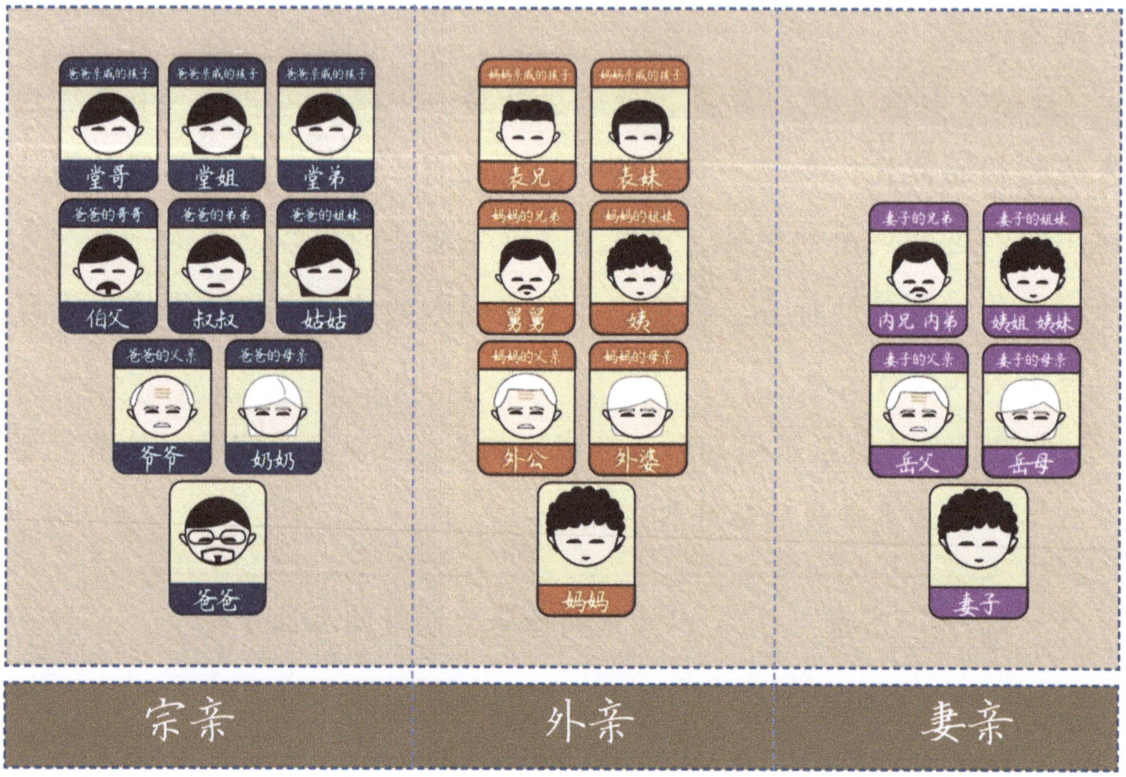

丈夫或妻子一样称呼爸爸、妈妈。丈夫的父母对外人称儿子的妻子为“儿媳”，妻子的父母对外人称女儿的丈夫为“女婿、姑爷”。

夫妻之间的称呼，古代和现在差异很大。古时候，丈夫当面称妻子为“夫人、娘子”，妻子当面称丈夫为“夫君、相公”。但丈夫对外人会称自己的妻子为“贱内、拙荆”，以表示一种谦虚。到了现在，夫妻之间的称呼变得简单了，可以直呼名字，也可以用比较亲切的“老公、老婆”。对外人则称为自己的“爱人”，也可以分别称为“先生”或“太太”。

兄弟姐妹如果各自结婚了，他们的丈夫或妻子之间的关系，也有特殊的说法。“妯娌”，指的是兄弟各自妻子之间的关系，“连襟”则是姐妹各自丈夫之间的关系。

听到这里，你恐怕已经糊涂了，但这还只是一个中国人最基本的亲属关系，如果再加上其他各类亲戚，那就更复杂了。从称谓中，我们能感受到中国人对“家”的关注。家庭中每一个成员都会在家族坐标中获得一个明确的定位、一个专门的称谓。对家族和血缘的重视是中国传统文化非常重要的特点。

生词 Words and expressions

1	禁忌	jìnjì	taboo
2	细节	xìjié	detail
3	称谓	chēngwèi	form of address; appellation
4	血缘	xuèyuán	blood relationship; ties of blood

5	纽带	niǔdài	link; bond
6	妯娌	zhóuli	wives of brothers
7	连襟	liánjīn	husbands of sisters
8	糊涂	hútu	muddled
9	坐标	zuòbiāo	coordinate

练习 Exercises

1 阅读课文，中国人的亲属称谓跟以下哪些方面密切相关？（　　）

Read the text and find out the aspect that is closely related with Chinese kinsfolk appellation. (Multiple Answer Question)

A. 血缘
- Blood relationship.

B. 身份
- Identity.

C. 地位
- Status.

D. 婚姻
- Marriage.

2 阅读课文，关于中国的亲属称谓，下面哪个描述是错误的？（　　）

Read the text and find out the wrong description on Chinese kinsfolk appellation.

A. 在称呼平辈时，爸爸兄弟家的孩子，是“堂”亲
- When referring to people of the same generation, the children of the father's brother's family are the *tangqin* (堂亲，cousins).

B. 当着丈夫父母的面，妻子要称呼他们为“公公”和“婆婆”
- In the presence of the husband's parents, the wife should call them *gonggong*（公公, father-in-law）and *popo*（婆婆, mother-in-law）.

C. “贱内、拙荆”是一种谦虚的称呼方式
- *Jiannei* (贱内) and *zhuojing* (拙荆) is a modest way of addressing his own wife.

D. “妯娌”指的是两个兄弟各自妻子之间的关系
- *Zhouli* (妯娌) refers to the relationship between the wives of two brothers.

3 请将相对应的亲属称谓连线。

Match the kinsfolk appellations with the corresponding persons.

爸爸的哥哥 Dad's elder brother	女婿、姑爷 *Nüxu, guye*
妈妈的兄弟 Mom's brother	伯伯 *Bobo*
丈夫对外人称呼妻子的父母 A husband refers to his wife's parents	贱内、拙荆 *Jiannei, zhuojin*
父母对外人称呼女儿的丈夫 Parents refer to their daughter's husband	连襟 *Lianjin*
古时候丈夫对外称呼自己的妻子 In ancient times, a husband refered to his wife	舅舅 *Jiujiu*
两个姐妹各自丈夫之间的关系 The relationship between the husbands of sisters	岳父、岳母 *Yuefu, yuemu*

10.4 敬称与谦称

Honorific and Modest Titles

英文课文见P158

除了家族里的称谓，社会上不同的角色和地位也会有一些特殊的称谓。

在古代社会，皇帝的地位至高无上，官员们则通过官职来区分地位，普通百姓绝对不可以称呼皇帝和官员的名字。同样，地位低的人和年轻人也不可以直呼地位高的人和年长者的名字。对皇帝，可以用“陛下、圣上、皇上”这些敬称，皇帝则自称“朕、孤、寡人”。官员对皇帝自称“臣、微臣”。职位低的官员称呼职位高的官员时，一般称呼对方的官职再加“大人”，自称“下官、小人”。而普通百姓则把所有官员都称为“大人”，自称“小人”。对现代人来说，这些复杂的称呼也许是不可思议的，但对古人来说则绝对不可以用错，否则就破坏了礼。

在《徐显卿宦绩图》中可以看到职位低的官员一般下跪陈述事情

In *Picture of Xu Xianqing's Official Career*, junior officials can be seen kneeling to state the case.

今天，如果你对一个人表示尊敬，可能会称呼男性为某先生、称呼女性为某女士。但这种称呼方式在中国传统称谓中是不存在的。古代的“先生”和“师傅”指的都是老师。现在称呼他人“王先生”、“张师傅”，也许只是表示尊重或客气，对方可不一定是老师。

西方人有时可能会直接称呼自己父母或者长者的名字，这在中国传统文化中也是绝对不允许的。在传统社会，当面称呼自己的父母用“父亲、母亲”或“父亲大人、母亲大人”；在别人面前称呼自己父母为“家父、家母”；称呼对方父母时，用“令尊、令堂”。现在，很多年长者仍习惯用这些敬称，但在年轻人中已逐渐变成“爸爸、妈妈”这样简单的称呼了。

与敬称相对的是谦称，这是在称呼自己时表示谦虚的一种称法。比如古代男人自称“不才、在下、晚生”；女人自称“妾身、奴家”等。称呼自己的孩子，也会用谦称，比如“犬子、小女”。上面提到的“小人、下官、微臣”等也都可以看成是谦称。今天，谦称用得少了，只有在非常正式的场合，偶尔会听到“在下”这样的谦称。

生词 Words and expressions

1	敬称	jìngchēng	honorific title
2	谦称	qiānchēng	modest title; self-abasing term

3	至高无上	zhìgāo-wúshàng	supreme
4	官职	guānzhí	official position
5	陛下	bìxià	Your Majesty
6	圣上	shèngshàng	Your Majesty
7	朕	zhèn	I; my (*used exclusively by the emperor in feudal China*)
8	孤	gū	I; my (*used exclusively by the emperor in feudal China*)
9	寡人	guǎrén	I; my (*used exclusively by the emperor in feudal China*)
9	微臣	wēichén	humble servant
10	某	mǒu	some; certain
11	吻合	wěnhé	to coincide
12	偶尔	ǒu'ěr	occasionally

练习 Exercises

1 阅读课文，下面哪项不是对皇帝的敬称？（　　）

Read the text and find out the item that is not an honorific title for the emperor.

A. 陛下
Bixia.

B. 皇上
Huangshang.

C. 寡人
Guaren.

D. 圣上
Shengshang.

2 阅读课文，关于敬称和谦称，下面描述正确的是哪一项？（　　）

Read the text and find out the right description on the honorific and modest titles.

A. 古代老百姓自称“小人”，谦称所有官员为“大人”

- People in ancient times called modestly themselves *xiaoren*, and called respectfully all officials *daren*.

B. “先生”和“师傅”指的都是老师。

- Both *xiansheng* and *shifu* refer to teachers.

C. 当着对方的面称呼对方父母时，用“令尊、令堂”。

- One would call others' parents *lingzun* and *lingtang* in his/her face.

D. “在下”是古代男子对自己的敬称。

- *Zaixia* was an ancient man's honorific title for himself.

3 阅读课文，下面哪项称呼不是谦称？（　　）

Read the text and find out the one that is not a modest title.

A. 圣上

- *Shengshang*.

B. 在下

- *Zaixia*.

C. 小女

- *Xiaonü*.

D. 微臣

- *Weichen*.

4 思考题：想想自己国家有哪些敬称和谦称？它们有什么样的使用场合和用法？

Are there any honorific and modest titles in your country? When are they used and what are the rules in using them?

10.5 家讳与国讳

The Family Taboo and National Taboo

英文课文见P159

在中国还有一种有趣的现象，叫避讳。中国人在称呼他人时，为了表示尊敬，要避免说出地位高者或年长者的名字，因此也叫名讳。避讳主要有国讳和家讳：国讳是回避当朝各代帝王的名字，家讳是回避本家族长辈的名字。

唐太宗李世民
Li Shimin, Emperor Taizong in Tang Dynasty

国讳是皇帝本人都要遵守的避讳。比如中国第一个皇帝秦始皇的父亲名“子楚”，所以，秦统一中国以后就把“楚”这个地方改称为“荆”。现在长江中游的湖北一带，仍被人称为荆楚之地。唐太宗李世民①的名字中有个“民”字，于是原来的政府部门“民部”从此就被改称为“户部”了。在古代，如果不注意帝王的名讳，可能获重罪，可能坐牢，甚至招来杀身之祸。

家讳，其实是国讳的一种延伸，也称为私讳。正如刚才在敬称中提到的，中国人直接称呼自己父母或长辈的姓名，会被看成是失礼的行为。唐代大诗人杜甫的父亲名叫“闲”，因此，杜甫写了一辈子的诗，传到今天的就有一千四百多首——却没在诗中用过一个“闲”字。

到了现代，虽然严格的名讳基本消失了，但避讳的思想在中国人的称呼规则中依然有着潜移默化的影响。

注释 Note

① 唐太宗李世民：唐朝第二位皇帝，626–649年在位，是中国历史上重要的政治家、战略家、军事家。

Li Shimin, Emperor Taizong in Tang Dynasty: He was the second emperor of the Tang Dynasty and had reigned from 626 to 649. He was an important statesman, strategist, and militarist in Chinese history.

生词 Words and expressions

1	回避	húibì	to avoid
2	遵守	zūnshǒu	to follow; to abide by
3	坐牢	zuòláo	to be imprisoned; to be in jail
4	杀身之祸	shāshēngzhīhuò	fatal disaster
5	延伸	yánshēn	to extend; to stretch
6	潜移默化	qiányí-mòhuà	to be unconsciously influenced

练习 Exercises

1 阅读第十课课文，判断下面的表达是否正确。

Read Lesson 10 and tell whether the following statements are true or false.

1）现代中国社会以自由恋爱为主，门当户对的思想已经消失了。（　　）

■ In modern Chinese society, love marriage is the norm , and the idea of equal status between families has disappeared.

2）中国传统婚礼要挑选黄道吉日，比如有数字“6”或“8”的日子。（　　）

■ Traditional Chinese weddings would choose ecliptic auspicious days, such as the sixth or eighth days.

3）中国传统的丧葬方式有土葬、火葬、天葬、水葬等，但最常见的是土葬。（　　）

■ Traditional Chinese burial methods include burial in the earth, cremation, celestial burial, and water burial, and the most common one is burial in the earth.

4）清明节的习俗是扫墓，一般是在每年的7月5日。（　　）

■ It is a custom to sweep the grave on Tomb-Sweeping Day, that is, usually on July 5th every year.

5）复杂的亲属称谓体现了中国人对家族和血缘的重视。（　　）

■ The complex kinsfolk appellation reflects Chinese people's emphasis on family and consanguinity.

6）“小人、下官、微臣、在下”等都是谦称。（　　）

■ *Xiaoren*, *xiaguan*, *weichen* and *zaixia* are all modest titles.

7）国讳和家讳都是名讳，都是为了表示尊敬。（　　）

■ The national taboo and family taboo are both name taboos to show respect.

2 阅读课文，下面不属于国讳的是哪项？（　　）

Read the text and find out the one that is not a national taboo.

A. 秦始皇改“楚”为“荆”

■ Qinshihuang changed "Chu (楚)" to "Jing (荆)".

B. 唐朝改“民部”为“户部”

- In Tang Dynasty, the name for *Minbu* (literally, "Ministry of Households") was changed to *Hubu* (literally, "Ministry of Revenue").

C. 杜甫的诗中从没用过一个“闲”字

- Du Fu had never used the character "xian (闲)" in his poems.

D. 汉光武帝名刘秀，一度把秀才改为“茂才”

- Because Emperor Guangwu's name was Liu Xiu, so "秀才 (scholar)" was changed to "茂才" for a period of time.

3 阅读课文，关于家讳的叙述不正确的是哪个？（　　）

Read the text and find out the wrong description about family taboo.

A. 家讳又称为私讳，是国讳的一种延伸

- The family taboo is also called private taboo. It is an extended use of national taboo.

B. 家讳是避免说出家族长辈的名字

- The family taboo is to avoid saying the names of the elders in the family.

C. 如果没有直接称呼本家族长辈的名字，会招来杀身之祸

- Not avoiding using the names of the elders in your family may bring you fatal disaster.

D. 不直接称呼自己父母或长辈的姓名，是符合礼的行为

- It is a kind of etiquette not to call the name of your own parents or the elderly in the family.

4 思考题：想想自己国家有哪些称谓方面的避讳？

Think about the taboos in appellation in your country.

小结 Summary

可以看到，无论是生死、婚姻这样的大事，还是日常称呼这样的小事，都有其特定的规范。这些规范融合在一起，形成了中国人的“礼数”，也潜移默化地塑造了中国人的性格，指导着中国人的行为。

As we see, there are specific norms on both major events, such as birth, death and marriage, and trivial matters, such as daily addressing. The rituals by Chinese people are the integration of those specific norms. They have subtly influenced and shaped Chinese people's character and guided their behaviors.

11

人才选用有尺度

Regulations on Talent Selection

热身 Warm-up

我们说家讳是国讳的延伸。其实不仅如此，中国人的家与国之间有着非同一般的密切关系，家庭或家族的管理模式与国家治理往往一脉相承。可以说，家是小国，国是大家，这一特征被称为家国同构。而礼，则可以看成是中国先人对社会秩序所寄托的一种理想，它渗透在日常生活、生老病死、婚丧嫁娶、人际关系的方方面面，约束和规范着人们的行为。而在国家层面，3000多年前西周的周公旦写成《周礼》一书，将“礼”上升为一种国家治理的目标。为了达到“礼治”，一代代国家治理者总结前人的智慧，形成了中华民族独特的选人用人机制，也创造出生发于本土的完整而成熟的国家管理模式。

We say that the family taboo is the extention of the national taboo, but it's actually more than that. Home is closely related to country to Chinese people. Keeping a family is often in line with governing a country. Family is an epitomized country and country is a big family. This is the isomorphism of family and country. *Li*, on one hand, is an ideal that Chinese ancestors placed on social order since it regulates people's behaviors in all aspect of daily life, including birth, death, marriage, funeral, and interpersonal relationship; and on the other hand, it is a goal of national governance, and influenced the state administrators of subsequent dynasties and generations since it was written in *The Rites of Zhou* by Zhougong Dan in Western Zhou Dynasty more than 3,000 years ago. In order to achieve the rule of ritual, China has formed a unique talent selection system and a complete and mature native national governance system with the wisdom of generations of state governors.

- 想一想，自己国家是怎样选拔人才的？
  How to select talents in your country?

11.1 举孝廉与九品中正制

Recommending People Noted for Filial Piety and Morality and the Nine-Rank System of Meritocracy of Selecting Officials

英文课文见P160

国家治理，首先得有人才。自古以来的国家管理者都注重人才的选拔，《周礼》①中就有相关的记载，“三年则大比”，即三年考核一次，挑选贤能的人补充到管理者队伍中。到了2000年前的汉朝，国家集中、统一、稳定，国家管理者们实行一种称为“察举”的选人用人制度，把品德高尚、能力出众的人推荐给国家。考察的名目有很多，其中最重要的是“孝廉”，意思是孝顺父母、做事公正，拥有这些品质的人才能成为官员。把孝顺放在最重要的位置，体现了中国古代国家治理中家的地位。

黄香是东汉时期官员，“扇枕温衾”是讲他小时候孝顺父母的故事。

Huang Xiang was an official in the Eastern Han Dynasty. “Fanning the pillow and warming the blanket” tells a story about his filial piety to his parents when he was young.

虽然推选那些孝顺的、品德好的人来做官符合“礼治”②的要求，但实际操作时，真正被举为孝廉的往往是贵族或富豪人家的子弟，平民百姓很难进入到国家治理体系里。到了三国时期，魏文帝曹丕[3]推出了任人唯贤的九品中正制[4]，目的当然是希望能够尽快地获得人才，但很快，这一制度也沦为世家大族把持重要官位的手段。

注释 Notes

①《周礼》：儒家经典，相传由西周时期的著名政治家周公旦所著。

The Rites of Zhou: It is a Confucian classic, which according to legend is written by Zhougong Dan, a famous statesman in Western Zhou Dynasty.

② 礼治：春秋战国时期儒家主张以礼治国的思想学说，与“法治”相对应，倡导以“礼”的原则治理国家。

The rule of ritual: It is an ideology advocated by Confucian school in the Spring and Autumn Period and the Warring States Period. In contrast with the “rule of law”, the “rule of ritual” advocates governing the country with the principle of ritual.

③ 魏文帝曹丕（187—226）：曹魏开国皇帝，魏武帝曹操之子，三国时期的政治家、文学家。

Cao Pi (187-226), Emperor Wen of Wei Kingdom: He is the founding emperor of Cao Wei. He is the son of Cao Cao, Emperor Wu of Wei Kingdom. He is a statesman and litterateur of the Three Kingdoms Period.

④ 九品中正制：魏晋南北朝时期重要的选官制度。按照“家世、道德、才能”的标准将人才分为九等，分别是上上、上中、上下、中上、中中、中下、下上、下中、下下。

The nine-rank system of meritocracy: It was an important imperial system of selecting officials during the Wei, Jin, Southern and Northern Dynasties. Talents were divided into nine classes according to their family backgrounds, morals and talents: upper-up (上上), upper-middle (上中), upper-low (上下), middle-up (中上), middle-middle (中中), middle-low (中下), lower-up (下上), lower-middle (下中), and lower-low (下下).

生词 Words and expressions

1	选拔	xuǎnbá	to select
2	记载	jìzǎi	to record
3	考核	kǎohé	to examine; to check
3	贤能	xiánnéng	able and virtuous personage
4	品德	pǐndé	morality
5	高尚	gāoshàng	noble; lofty
6	出众	chūzhòng	outstanding; exceptional
7	名目	míngmù	names of things; items
8	孝廉	xiàolián	filial and incorrupt
9	体系	tǐxì	system; setup
10	任人唯贤	rènrén-wéixián	to appoint people on their merits
11	世家大族	shìjiā dàzú	aristocratic family
12	把持	bǎchí	to control; to keep under control
13	手段	shǒuduàn	means; method

练习 Exercises

1 阅读课文，下面哪种书籍中有关于人才选拔的记载？（　　）

Read the text and find out which of the following books records the selection of talents.

A. 《周礼》
- *The Rites of Zhou.*

B. 《诗经》
- *The Book of Songs.*

C. 《楚辞》
- *The Song of Chu*

D. 《离骚》
- *Lisao*

2 阅读课文，在汉朝什么样的人可能被选拔为官员？（ ）

Read the text and find out people that might be selected as officials in Han Dynasty.

A. 能力出众的人
- Outstanding people.

B. 平民百姓
- Common people.

C. 知识渊博的人
- Knowledgeable people.

D. 孝顺父母的人
- People who are filial to their parents.

3 阅读课文，关于九品中正制，下面描述不正确的是哪项？（ ）

Read the text and find out the wrong description about the nine-rank system of meritocracy.

A. 是由曹丕推出的人才选拔方法
- It is the talent selection method introduced by Cao Pi.

B. 是魏晋时期重要的选官制度
- It is an important official selection system in the Wei and Jin dynasties.

C. 目的是选拔出孝顺和公正的人成为官员
- The purpose is to select talents with filial piety and justice to become officials.

D. 选拔的标准是“家世、道德、才能”
- The criteria for selection are "family background, morality and talent".

4 思考题：查阅资料，谈谈“察举制”和“九品中正制”的优缺点。

Search the information and compare the "recommendatory system" with the "nine-rank system" of meritocracy in official selection.

11.2 千年科举及其影响

The Imperial Examination Lasting for a Thousand of Years and Its Influence

英文课文见P161

在一个庞大的国家，如何才能真正获得人才？这一问题随着时间的推移变得越来越严峻。在这样的背景下，到了1400年前的隋唐时期，国家管理者们终于推出了一个与以往选人机制完全不同的方案，这就是科举制。在未来漫长的历史中，这一制度不断被改造、调整、完善，一直沿用到1905年才被废除。

科举制打破了豪门大族对官位的把持，为普通平民开辟了一条上升

南京江南贡院的号舍遗址。号舍是科举时代考生考试的地方。

Haoshe ruins in Jiangnan Gongyuan, Nanjing. Haoshe was the place where examinees took examinations in the imperial examination era.

的道路，所以有唐诗说："朝为田舍郎，暮登天子堂。"早晨还在农田里干活儿，晚上就登上了官位。在上层士族和平民百姓之间，终于有了这样一条通道，它虽然并不宽广，却始终畅通，将新鲜血液源源不断输送到国家人才体系中，从而使整个管理机制不会完全僵化。

科举制实行了1000多年，积累了极为丰富的人才选拔和考试制度的经验和智慧，今天中国的高考和公务员考试的许多做法依然能看到科举考试的影子。科举制不仅深刻影响了日本、韩国、越南等东亚和东南亚国家，甚至西方建立文官制度也对此有所借鉴。

通过一套成熟的选拔机制，人才被培养和挑选出来，其最终目的是充实到国家的组织机构中。所以，中国的读书人自古就有"学而优则仕"①的观念，也有"修身齐家治国平天下"②的理想，他们渴望在国家的官僚体制中被认可，并步步提升。

注释 Notes

① 学而优则仕：出自《论语·子张》，意思是学习还有余力就去做官。后指学习优异的人可以提拔当官。
He who excels in learning would end up being an official: It comes from "*Zizhang*" in *The Analects of Confucius*. Later it referred to promoting those with excellent academic performance to office.

② 修身齐家治国平天下：出自儒家经典《礼记·大学》，意思是提高自身修养，管理好家庭事务，治理好所在的地区，最后使全国安宁。
Cultivating both the body and spirit, conducting both the family and the state, placating the world under the sky: It is from "*Daxue*" in *The Book of Rites*, a Confucian classic, meaning to improve self-cultivation, manage household affairs, administer the state and bring peace to the nation.

生词 Words and expressions

1	庞大	pángdà	huge; enormous
2	推移	tuīyí	to pass; to develop
3	严峻	yánjùn	severe; austere
4	改造	gǎizào	to transform; to reform
5	废除	fèichú	to abolish; to abrogate
6	豪门	háomén	rich and powerful family
7	开辟	kāipì	to open up
8	士族	shìzú	(in feudal society) influential family of many generations
9	源源不断	yuányuán-búduàn	continuously
10	僵化	jiānghuà	to become rigid; to ossify
11	充实	chōngshí	substantial; rich
12	官僚	guānliáo	bureaucrat
13	认可	rènkě	to approve; to accept
14	提升	tíshēng	to promote; to improve

练习 Exercises

1 阅读课文，以下科举制的起止朝代正确的是哪一个？（　　）

Read the text and find out when the imperial examination was adopted and ended.

A. 隋朝起，宋朝止

From Sui Dynasty to Song Dynasty.

B. 隋朝起，明朝止

- From Sui Dynasty to Ming Dynasty.

C. 唐朝起，元朝止

- From Tang Dynasty to Yuan Dynasty.

D. 隋朝起，清朝止

- From Sui Dynasty to Qing Dynasty.

2 阅读课文，关于科举制的描述不正确的是哪一项？（　　）

Read the text and find out the wrong description about the imperial examination system.

A. 为普通平民开辟了一条上升的道路

- It opened up an upward path for common people.

B. 使国家的整个管理机制不会完全僵化

- Thanks to the imperial examination, the national governance mechanism was not completely rigid.

C. 积累了丰富的人才选拔和考试制度的经验和智慧

- It pooled rich experience and wisdom in talent selection and examination system.

D. 今天中国的高考和公务员考试依然采用科举制

- Today, China's college entrance examination and civil service examination still adopt the imperial examination.

3 阅读课文，从诗句“朝为田舍郎，暮登天子堂”中，我们可以了解古代中国读书人的什么观念？（　　）

Read the text and find out the ancient Chinese scholars' ideas in the poem "A farmer working in the fields in the early morning, became an official in the imperial palace in the evening".

A. 学而优则仕

- Officialdom is the natural outlet for good scholars.

B. 修身

- Cultivate his own moral character.

C. 齐家

- Bring his family together to be united.

D. 孝顺

- Filial piety.

④ 思考题：想想自己国家是怎么选拔人才的？有什么特点？

How are officials or talents selected in your country? What are the characteristics?

11.3 从三公九卿到三省六部

From the Three Councillors and Nine Ministers of the State to the Three Departments and Six Ministries

英文课文见P162

公元前221年，秦始皇统一中国，从那时起到1911年的2000多年里，中国大地上实行的都是中央集权的帝制统治，而与它配套的是一套成熟的官僚制度。

在中央，秦汉时期实行“三公九卿制”。“三公”的说法古已有之，指的是管理体制中最高的三种官职，但在不同朝代有不同的职位；九卿指中央的各个重要官员，在各个朝代也并不统一。所以“三公九卿”更多的是秦朝对以往各国治理经验的制度总结。

中央官制运行到隋唐，形成了一套组织严密的体系——三省六部制。三省指中书省[①]、门下省[②]、尚书省[③]，六部指尚书省下属的吏部[④]、户部[⑤]、礼部[⑥]、兵部[⑦]、刑部[⑧]、工部[⑨]。三省六部制在此后的朝代更迭中不断调整、改造，逐渐变得更为完备、细致、成熟，一直到清朝末年才彻底废止，其机制运行达到了一个很高的水平。

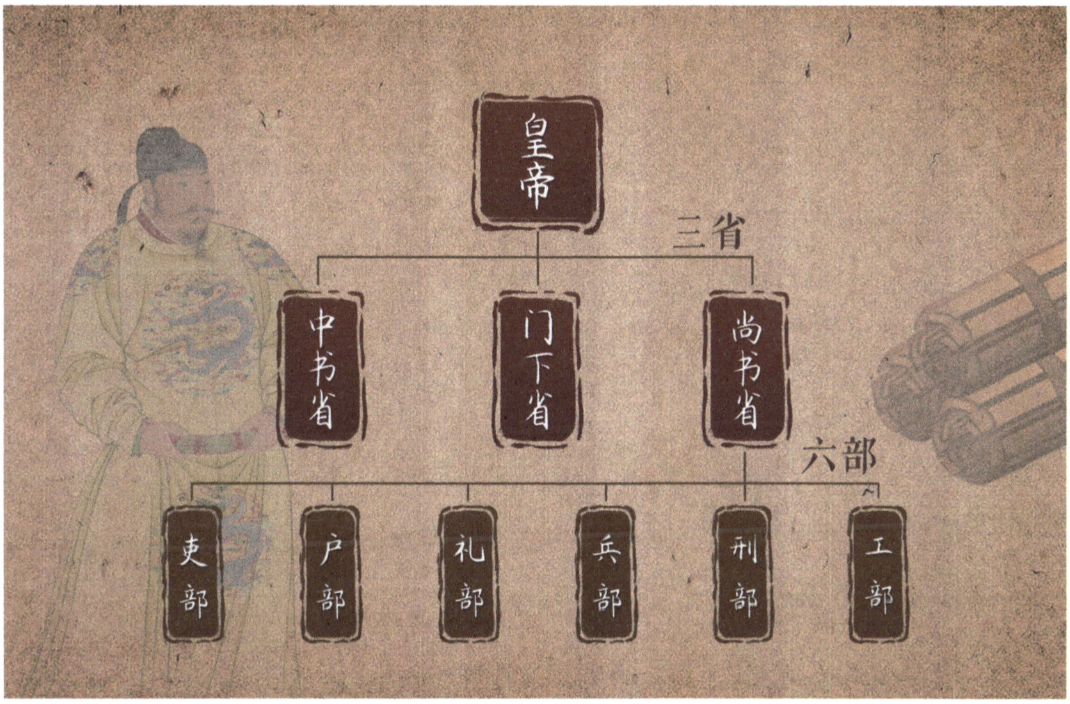

注释 Notes

① 中书省：古代中央政府最高权力机构之一，是掌管机要、发布政令的机构。
Zhongshu Department: It was one of the highest authorities of ancient central government. It was the organization that controled confidentiality and issued government orders.

② 门下省：古代中央政府最高权力机构之一，负责审查诏令的机构。
Menxia Department: It was one of the highest authorities of ancient central government. It was responsible of reviewing imperial edicts..

③ 尚书省：古代中央政府最高权力机构之一，负责执行诏令的机构。
Shangshu Department: It was one of the highest authorities of ancient central government. It was responsible of carrying out imperial edicts.

④ 吏部：中国古代官署，掌管全国官吏的任免、考课、升降、调动等事务。

Ministry of Official Personnel Affairs: It was the ancient Chinese government office in charge of the appointment, dismissal, examinations, promotion, transfer of officials throughout the country.

⑤ 户部：中国古代官署，掌管户籍财经的机构。

Ministry of Revenue: It was the ancient Chinese government office in charge of household registration and finance.

⑥ 礼部：中国古代官署，管理全国学校事务及科举考试、藩属及外国往来事务。

Ministry of Rites: It was the ancient Chinese government office in charge of national school affairs, imperial examinations, and exchanges between vassal states and foreign countries.

⑦ 兵部：中国古代官署，掌管选用武官以及与兵籍、军械、发布军令等相关的事务。

Ministry of War: It was the ancient Chinese government office in charge of the selection of military officers, military status, ordnance, military orders, etc.

⑧ 刑部：中国古代官署，主管全国刑罚政令及审核刑名的机构。

Ministry of Punishments: It was the ancient Chinese government office in charge of national penal decrees and review of criminals.

⑨ 工部：中国古代官署，掌管营造工程事项的机构。

Ministry of Works: It was the ancient Chinese government office in charge of construction projects.

生词 Words and expressions

1	集权	jíquán	centralization of state power
2	配套	pèitào	to match; to assort
3	中央	zhōngyāng	The highest leading body of state power
4	运行	yùnxíng	to run; to operate

4	严密	yánmì	tight; close
5	更迭	gēngdié	to change; to alternate
6	细致	xìzhì	careful; meticulous
7	废止	fèizhǐ	to abolish

练习 Exercises

1 阅读课文，“六部”中的“户部”主管什么事务？（　　）

Read the text and find out the affairs that Ministry of Revenue was in charge of.

A. 官员选拔
- Official selection.

B. 工程建设
- Project construction.

C. 户籍财政
- Household registration and revenue.

D. 外交往来
- Foreign exchanges.

2 阅读课文，科举考试由哪个机构负责？（　　）

Read the text and find out the agency that was responsible for the imperial examination.

A. 户部
- Ministry of Revenue.

B. 吏部
- Ministry of Official Personnel Affairs.

C. 礼部
- Ministry of Rites.

D. 工部
- Ministry of Works.

3 阅读课文，关于“三公九卿”和“三省六部”，下列哪个说法不正确？（　　）

Read the text and find out the wrong description about the "Three Councillors and Nine Minsiters of the State" and the "Three Departments and Six Ministries".

A. “三公九卿”是秦汉时期实行的制度

■ "Three Councillors and Nine Ministers to the State" was a system in Qin and Han dynasties.

B. “三公”的说法是从秦朝时开始使用的

■ The term “Three Councillors” has been used since Qin Dynasty.

C. “三公九卿”在不同朝代有不同的官职

■ "Three Councillors and Nine Ministers to the State" were different in official position in different dynasties.

D. “三省六部”比“三公九卿”更完善、严密

■ "Three Departments and Six Ministries" were more complete and rigorous than "Three Councillors and Nine Ministers".

4 1200年前，如果一个国家要派使节到唐朝，将由哪个机构负责接待？（　　）

If a country wanted to send envoys to Chang'an, the capital of the Tang Dynasty 1,200 years ago, which institution would be responsible for receiving them?

A. 兵部

■ Ministry of War.

B. 工部

■ Ministry of Works.

C. 礼部

■ Ministry of Rites.

D. 户部

■ Ministry of Revenue.

11.4 从郡县制到行省制

From the System of Prefectures and Counties to the System of Provincial Governance

英文课文见P163

早在秦始皇统一中国之前，大多数地方就已经在实行郡县制。秦朝一统天下后，继续沿用郡县二级制，地方官员由中央任免，地方处于

中央的管辖之下。到东汉后期又形成了州、郡、县三级制。此后无论是二级制还是三级制，中央对地方的行政管理模式都具有相似性，尤其是“县”级机构，沿用2000多年，至今仍是国家基础行政单位。

元朝开始实行行省制，即中央由中书省总管国家事务，而它的派出机构——行中书省管理地方行政。行省制的确立，形成了中国现代地方行政区划的雏形，虽然明朝对各大行省改称为布政使司，但习惯上仍称呼为“省”。从此，“省”这一称法一直是中国最高一级地方行政区划的名称，并沿用至今。

在1330年的元朝行政地图中已采用行省制。审图号：GS(2006)380号

The administrative map of Yuan Dynasty in 1330 has adopted the system of provincial governance.

生词 Words and expressions

1	郡县	jùnxiàn	the system of prefectures and counties
2	沿用	yányòng	continue to use

3	任免	rènmiǎn	to appoint and remove
4	管辖	guǎnxiá	to have jurisdiction over; to administer
5	行政	xíngzhèng	administration
6	区划	qūhuà	division into districts
7	雏形	chúxíng	embryonic form

练习 Exercises

1 阅读第十一课的课文，判断下面的表达是否正确。
Read Lesson 11 and tell whether the following statements are true or false.

1）汉朝实行一种称为"察举"的选人用人制度，最重要的标准是"孝廉"。 （ ）
- In Han Dynasty, recommendatory system was implemented in selecting and employing people, and filial piety and morality was the most important criterion.

2）科举制在中国实行了2000多年。 （ ）
- The imperial examination has been implemented in China for more than 2,000 years.

3）科举制打破了豪门大族对官位的把持，为平民百姓开辟了一条改变命运的道路。 （ ）
- The imperial examination broke the control of the rich and powerful family on official positions, and opened up a path for common people to change their fate.

4）秦朝建立了第一个中央集权的帝制统治的国家。 （ ）
- Qin Dynasty was the first power-centralized imperial state in Chinese history.

5）"三公九卿"和"三省六部"都是为了皇帝专权而设置的。 （ ）
- Both the "Three Councillors and Nine Minsiters of the State" and the "Three Departments and Six Ministries" were set up for the emperor's dictatorship.

6）"县"作为国家基础行政单位有2000多年的历史了。 （ ）
- "County" has been the basic administrative unit of China for more than 2,000 years.

2 阅读课文，什么是秦朝的基础行政单位？（　　）

Read the text and find out the basic administrative unit of Qin Dynasty.

A. 郡
- Prefecture.

B. 县
- County.

C. 城
- City.

D. 乡
- Township.

3 阅读课文，从哪个朝代起，省成为中国最高一级地方行政区划的名称？（　　）

Read the text and find out since when province became the highest-level local administrative division in China.

A. 秦朝
- Qin Dynasty.

B. 汉朝
- Han Dynasty.

C. 元朝
- Yuan Dynasty.

D. 清朝
- Qing Dynasty.

小结 Summary

在这些制度之外，中国很早就有一套监察制度与官僚制度并行，用以监督或弹劾官员，以免造成权力的滥用。所以，虽然是中央集权，但并不意味着由皇帝一人决策，国家的治理仍然是一套复杂而有效的管理机制在起作用。

In addition to these systems, China has had also a supervisory system in parallel with the bureaucratic system for supervising or impeaching officials to avoid abuse of power. Therefore, centralization did not equal to monopolizing power of the emperor, and a complex and effective administrative mechanism was still at work in national governance.

主题：对外交往

12 来而不往非礼也

It's Impolite Not to Reciprocate

热身 Warm-up

中国有漫长的陆地边界和海洋边界，因此自古邻国众多，与其他国家的交往历史非常悠久。早在2000多年前，孔子就曾说过："有朋自远方来，不亦乐乎？"这表达了中国文化中对待客人的一种态度。中国自古就有"礼尚往来"的思想，认为互相之间探望对方，是一种有礼节的表现。所以，交往的礼仪也是礼文化中不可或缺的一部分。

China has broad frontiers on land and sea. So, for a long time, it has had many neighboring countries and a long history of contact with them. More than 2,000 years ago, Confucius said, "Is it not a pleasure when a friend comes from afar?", expressing the attitude toward entertaining guests in Chinese culture. Chinese people have always had the idea that "courtesy demands reciprocity" since ancient times and thought that it is a courstesy to visit each other. Thus, communication etiquette is also an indispensable part of ritual culture.

- 想一想，在自己的国家，与人交往有什么样的礼俗呢？
  What are the etiquettes and customs of communication in your country?

12.1 丝绸之路与贸易

Silk Road and Trade

英文课文见P164

敦煌壁画上的张骞出使西域

Zhang Qian went on a diplomatic mission to the Western Regions in Dunhuang frescoes.

丝绸之路，是一条著名的陆地贸易通道，在2000多年前的西汉时期形成，从当时中国的首都长安（现在陕西西安），一直到当时的罗马帝国。汉朝的丝绸、茶叶，以及冶炼、水利和丝织技术，通过这条通道向西方传播；西方的皮毛、宝石、香料等，则来到中国。因为当时从中国向西方运输的货物中，以丝绸制品的影响最大，所以这条路被称为丝绸之路。

从那时起到明朝的1500多年里，丝绸之路虽然时断时续，但一直是中国与欧亚其他国家来往的重要通道。在漫长的历史中，很多著名的历史人物都与这条道路有关。西汉官员张骞①，丝绸之路的开拓者；

唐朝名僧玄奘②，去印度游学并带回大量经文，影响了整个东亚的佛教；意大利商人马可·波罗③，在中国游历17年，把中国的故事传播到欧洲，激起了欧洲人对东方的热烈向往。我们可以想象一个丝绸之路上的场景，商人和学者骑着马，牵着骆驼，行走在沙漠和戈壁中，看到有水和树木的地方就停下来歇歇脚。这些有水的地方成为绿洲，慢慢地，一些绿洲成为了美丽的小城。著名的敦煌④就曾经是这样的美丽小城，它为后代留下了蔚为大观的敦煌壁画。

跟丝绸之路相对应的，还有海上丝绸之路。海上丝绸之路出现在2000多年前的秦汉时期，1000年前的宋朝是它的繁荣期。那时，瓷器逐渐成为主要的贸易货物，源源不断地运往海外。所以有人也把海上贸易的通道称为“陶瓷之路”。

借助贸易，中国的丝绸和瓷器不断运往其他国家；很多年后，这些精美的物品也融入了当地人的生活。与此同时，其他国家的各种货物也不断地来到中国，充实着中国人的生活。今天中国人餐桌上常见的西红柿、西瓜、番薯、胡萝卜、胡椒等，从名字就能判断出它们的来源——“西”“番”“胡”都有外来的意思。

注释 Notes

① 张骞（约前164－前114）：西汉杰出的外交家、旅行家、探险家，丝绸之路的开拓者。

Zhang Qian (about 164 BC–114 BC): He was an outstanding diplomat, traveler, explorer and pioneer of the Silk Road in Western Han Dynasty.

② 玄奘（602或600－664）：唐代高僧，中国汉传佛教四大佛经翻译家之一。629年，玄奘西行求法，往返十七年，行程五万里，带回大量重要的佛教经典著

作。《大唐西域记》详细记载了他的经历。

Xuanzang (602/600–664): He was an eminent monk in Tang Dynasty, one of the four major Buddhist scripture translators of Chinese Buddhism. In 629, Xuanzang went west to seek Dharma. He traveled 50,000 miles within 17 years. He had brought back a large number of important Buddhist classics. The book *The Great Tang Dynasty Record of the Western Regions* records his itinerary in detail.

③ 马可·波罗（约1254—1324）：意大利旅行家、商人，在中国游历了十七年，著有《马可·波罗游记》，这本书激起了欧洲人对东方的向往。

Marco Polo (about 1254–1324): He was an Italian traveler and businessman. He had traveled in China for 17 years and wrote *The Travels of Marco Polo*, which aroused European people's yearning for the mysterious Orient.

④ 敦煌：位于甘肃省，是中国历史文化名城。敦煌是丝绸之路的节点城市，以石窟和壁画闻名天下。

Dunhuang: It is located in Gansu Province, and it is a famous historical and cultural city in China. Dunhuang was a node city on the Silk Road, and it is famous for its grottoes and murals.

生词 Words and expressions

1	冶炼	yěliàn	to smelt
2	宝石	bǎoshí	gemstone
3	香料	xiāngliào	perfume; spice
4	游学	yóuxué	to study in some other place or abroad
5	经文	jīngwén	scriptures
6	向往	xiàngwǎng	to yearn for
7	场景	chǎngjǐng	scene

8	戈壁	gēbì	gobi; the Gobi Desert
9	歇脚	xiējiǎo	to stop on the way for a rest
10	绿洲	lǜzhōu	oasis
11	蔚为大观	wèiwéidàguān	to be indeed a splendid sight
12	借助	jièzhù	to have the aid of
13	融入	róngrù	to blend in; to integrate
14	番薯	fānshǔ	sweet potato

练习 Exercises

1 阅读课文，来往于丝绸之路和海上丝绸之路上的商品有哪些？［多选］（ ）

Read the text and find out the commodities on the Silk Road and Maritime Silk Road. (Multiple Answer Question)

A.

B.

C.

D.

2 阅读课文，丝绸之路不经过哪个城市？（　　）

Read the text and find out the city that was not on the Silk Road.

A. 长安
- Chang'an.

B. 罗马
- Rome.

C. 敦煌
- Dunhuang.

D. 南京
- Nanjing.

3 关于海上丝绸之路，下面哪个描述是不正确的？（　　）

Which description is incorrect about the Maritime Silk Road?

A. 形成于秦汉时期
- It was built in the Qin and Han dynasties.

B. 繁荣于宋朝
- It got prosperous in the Song dynasty.

C. 最主要的贸易货物是丝绸
- The main trade goods was silk.

D. 也被称为“陶瓷之路”
- It was also known as the "Ceramic Road".

4 查阅资料，以下哪种果蔬原产于中国？（　　）

Search the information and find out the fruit or vegetable native to China.

A.

B.

C.

D.

12.2 远航与外交

Long Voyages and International Relations

英文课文见P165

在2000多年前的战国时期，中国广阔的土地上有很多诸侯国，它们之间的交往非常频繁。但当时交通不发达，交往多在邻国之间展开。秦始皇统一中国以后，交往的范围也随之扩大。到了东汉，日本倭奴国王曾派使臣来中国，并接受了汉光武帝[1]“汉倭奴国王”金印[2]。在西边，东汉与大秦[3]也有互派使节的记载。

到了唐朝，经济繁荣，文化发达，东西方各国与中国的交往都很密切。日本曾13次派遣唐使[4]来中国学习文化和制度。中东地区的大食[5]派使者到中国的次数则超过了30次。

明朝时期，郑和[6]受皇帝派遣，七次出海，每次都率领庞大的船

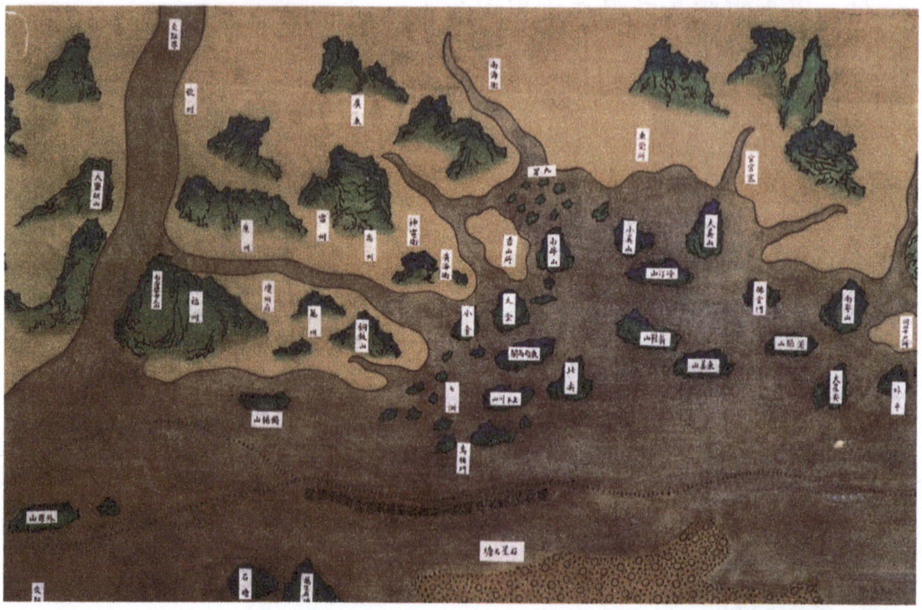

《郑和航海图》（局部）

Zheng He's Nautical Chart (partial)

队，到达东南亚、南亚、非洲等地区的各个国家。回国时，还邀请许多国家的国王和使臣到中国访问。“郑和下西洋”所体现出来的远航实力，在当时的世界上是无可比拟的。

郑和下西洋的贡献留在了《郑和航海图》⑦上，而对海洋的探索在明代海禁以后却衰落了。清朝时，中国开始采取更加严格的闭关锁国⑧政策，与国外的交往也就越来越少。

注释 Notes

① 汉光武帝：东汉开国皇帝刘秀（前5—公元57）。

Emperor Guangwu of Han Dynasty: Liu Xiu (5 BC–57 AD) was the founding emperor of the Eastern Han Dynasty.

② “汉倭奴国王”金印：东汉初年，日本列岛部落国王为借助强盛的汉帝国权威，派遣使者觐见汉光武帝。汉光武帝为嘉许其远来恭敬之情，授以金印，赐名以“倭”。

The “Han King of Wonu” gold official seal: In the early Eastern Han Dynasty, to seek shelter from the powerful Han Empire, the tribal king of the Japanese archipelagoes sent envoys to meet Emperor Guangwu of Han Dynasty. Emperor Guangwu granted them the name “Wo (倭)” and gave them a gold seal in honor of their coming from afar to show respect.

③ 大秦：中国古籍中对罗马帝国的称呼。

Daqin: It was an ancient name for the Roman Empire and the Near East.

④ 遣唐使：从七世纪初至九世纪末，日本为了学习中国文化，先后向唐朝派出十几次外交使团。

Envoys sent to Tang Dynasty: From the beginning of the seventh century to the end of the ninth century, Japan had sent a dozen of envoys to Tang Dynasty to learn Chinese culture.

⑤ 大食：中国史籍中唐宋时期对阿拉伯帝国的称呼。

Dashi: It was a Chinese term for Arabs during Tang and Song dynasties.

⑥ 郑和：明代航海家、外交家。1405年至1433年，郑和七次带领明朝船队下西洋，对中外经济、文化交往起到了非常积极的作用。

Zheng He: He was a navigator and diplomat in Ming Dynasty. Zheng He led the Ming fleet to the West seven times in 1405–1433. He played a very positive role in the economic and cultural exchanges between China and foreign countries.

⑦《郑和航海图》：约绘成于1425至1430年间。该图是对郑和下西洋航线的记录，也是世界上现存最早的航海图集。

Zheng He's Nautical Chart: It was drawn approximately between 1425 and 1430. It was a map record of Zheng He's voyages to the West Seas, and was the earliest surviving nautical atlas in the world.

⑧ 闭关锁国：指闭关自守、不与外界接触的一种国家政策。

Sealing itself off from foreign contact: It refers to a national policy that keeps the country closed and does not contact with the outside world.

生词 Words and expressions

1	广阔	guǎngkuò	vast; wide
2	频繁	pínfán	often; frequently
3	使臣	shǐchén	envoy
4	无可比拟	wúkěbǐnǐ	beyond comparison
5	探索	tànsuǒ	to explore
6	海禁	hǎijìn	ban on maritime trade or intercourse with foreign countries
7	衰落	shuāiluò	to decline

练习 Exercises

1. 阅读课文，“汉倭奴国王”金印是哪个中国皇帝赐给日本倭奴国王的？（ ）
Read the text and find out the Chinese emperor that granted the "Han King of Wonu".

A. 汉武帝
- Emperor Wu of Han Dynasty.

B. 汉光武帝
B. Emperor Guangwu of Han Dynasty.

C. 汉文帝
C. Emperor Wen of Han Dynasty.

D. 汉景帝
D. Emperor Jing of Han Dynasty.

2. 阅读课文，大食派使者到中国超过30次是在哪个朝代？（ ）
Read the text and find out the dynasty that Dashi came to China for more than 30 times.

A. 汉朝
- Han Dynasty.

B. 唐朝
- Tang Dynasty.

C. 宋朝
- Song Dynasty.

D. 清朝
- Qing Dynasty.

3. 查阅资料，关于“郑和下西洋”的描述不正确的是哪一项？（ ）
Search the information and find out the wrong description of Zheng He's voyages to the West Seas.

A. 郑和作为使者曾7次出使西洋
- Zheng He has been to the West Seas seven times as an envoy.

B. 郑和下西洋是中国古代规模最大、时间最久的海上航行
- Zheng He's voyages to the West Seas was the largest and longest maritime voyages in ancient China.

C. 郑和下西洋的目的是促进贸易往来
- The purpose of Zheng He's voyages to the West Seas was to promote trade.

D. 《郑和航海图》记录了郑和下西洋的航线

■ *Zheng He's Nautical Chart* records the route of Zheng He's voyages to the West Seas.

4 仔细观察，下面哪幅图描绘的是“郑和下西洋”的场景？（　　）

Look at the pictures and find out the one that depicts Zheng He's voyages to the West Seas.

A.

B.

C.

D.

12.3 文化的双向交流

Mutual Cultural Communication

英文课文见P165

古代中国与外国的文化交流，既有以佛教为代表的外来文化的传入，也包括中国对周边国家的影响。

佛教产生于公元前6世纪的古印度[①]，在西汉末年传入中国的中原地区，在南北朝时期得到发扬并达到鼎盛，现在我们看到的很多佛像和石窟，都是在那个时期建造的。唐朝时佛教依然盛行，其中有两位高僧在佛教的传播中贡献巨大。

第一位是玄奘，他历经艰辛到达当时的佛教圣地天竺[②]，拜访高僧，研究佛学，翻译经文，并带回大量佛教经典，对佛教在中国的发展起到了很大的推动作用。《大唐西域记》[③]记载了他一路上的见闻，是珍贵的历史文献。中国四大名著之一的《西游记》就是以他的经历为背景写成的。

另一位有名的高僧是鉴真[④]。他六次东渡日本才成功到达，并在日本居住了十年，传播佛教和中国文化。现在，日本仍然供奉着鉴真的雕像。

日本唐招提寺中的鉴真坐像

Jianzhen's sitting statue in Tangzhaoti Temple, Japan

到今天，佛教早已成为中国文化不可分割的一部分。很多词汇和成语都是从佛教中来的，比如“世界、大众、真相、不可思议、茅塞顿开、当头棒喝”等等。民间俗语中受佛教影响的内容也很多。

文化交流永远是双向的，在积极接

受并融合外来文化的同时，中国也不断地影响着周边国家，比如文字。今天，我们仍可以在日文中看到汉字，越南、韩国、朝鲜在100年前也都还在使用汉字，并形成了所谓的汉字文化圈⑤。在日语、韩语和越南语中，经常能听到一些与汉语发音相似的词语，因为它们都是从汉语中借走的。除此以外，在节日、中医中药、建筑风格等各个方面，中国对周边国家也都有很深的影响。

注释 Notes

① 古印度：这里特指古印度的迦毗罗卫国（今尼泊尔境内）。
Ancient India: Here it refers specifically to the Kapilavu Kingdom of ancient India (in the present-day Nepal).

②天竺：古代对印度和其他南亚次大陆国家的统称。
Tianzhu: It collectively referred to India and other countries in the South Asian Subcontinent in ancient times.

③《大唐西域记》：又称《西域记》，记载的是玄奘从长安出发西行游历西域的所见所闻。
The Great Tang Dynasty Records of the Western Regions: It is also known as *Records of the Western Regions* and records Xuanzang's travelling experience from Chang'an to the West.

④ 鉴真（688—763）：唐代高僧，日本律宗初祖，亦称“过海大师”“唐大和尚”。曾六次东渡，历经挫折，直到第六次航行才成功到达日本。鉴真在日本传播佛教和中国文化，也被日本人民奉为医药始祖。
Jianzhen (688–763): He was an eminent monk in Tang Dynasty. He was also known as"Sea-Crossing Master"or"the Great Tang Monk"in Japan. He was the founder of Japanese Vinaya school of Buddhism in Japan and tried six times to cross to Japan and at the last time he succeeded. Jianzhen spread Buddhism and Chinese culture in Japan. He was regarded as the founder of Japanese pharmaceutics.

⑤ 汉字文化圈：指曾有汉字书写历史并受到中国文化影响的国家，主要包括越南、朝鲜、韩国、新加坡、日本等国。

Sinosphere: It refers to countries with a history of writing Chinese characters and are influenced by China and Chinese culture, mainly including Vietnam, North Korea, South Korea, Singapore, Japan and so on.

生词 Words and expressions

1	双向	shuāngxiàng	two-way; bothway
2	发扬	fāyáng	to develop; to promote; to carry forward
3	鼎盛	dǐngshèng	in a period of great prosperity
4	盛行	shèngxíng	to prevail
5	历经	lìjīng	to go through
6	艰辛	jiānxīn	hardship
7	圣地	shèngdì	holy land
8	经典	jīngdiǎn	classic
9	分割	fēngē	to cut apart; to break up
10	真相	zhēnxiàng	truth
11	茅塞顿开	máosè-dùnkāi	to be enlightened all of a sudden
12	当头棒喝	dāngtóu-bànghè	a blow and a shout; a sharp warning
13	所谓	suǒwèi	so-called

练习 Exercises

1 阅读第十二课课文，判断下面的表达是否正确。

Read Lesson 12 and tell whether the following statements are true or false.

1）丝绸之路始于2000多年前的唐朝，起点是当时的首都长安。（ ）

- The Silk Road started more than 2,000 years ago from the capital Chang'an of Tang Dynasty then.

2）通过贸易往来，丝绸和陶瓷成为中国的代名词。（ ）

- Silk and ceramics became labels of China through trade.

3）唐朝是个开放的朝代，与各国交往都很密切。（ ）

- Tang Dynasty was an open dynasty which had close contact with all countries.

4）明朝时期，郑和受皇帝派遣，七次出海。（ ）

- In Ming Dynasty, Zheng He had been dispatched by the emperor to voyage to the West Seas for seven times.

5）清朝时期，中国仍然与外国保持频繁的贸易往来。（ ）

- China still maintained frequent trade contacts with foreign countries in Qing Dynasty.

6）唐朝高僧玄奘和鉴真对佛教的传播贡献巨大。（ ）

- Xuanzang and Jianzhen, the eminent monks of Tang Dynasty, have made great contributions to the spread of Buddhism.

2 阅读课文，四大名著中哪部是基于玄奘西行的经历写成的？（ ）

Read the text and find out the one of the four classic works based on Xuanzang's experience of traveling to the west.

A. 《三国演义》

- *Romance of the Three Kingdoms.*

B. 《水浒传》

- *Outlaws of the Marshes.*

C. 《西游记》

- *Journey to the West.*

D. 《红楼梦》

- *Dream of the Red Chambers.*

3 阅读课文，下面哪个国家不属于汉字文化圈？（　　）

Read the text and find out the country that does not belong to the Sinophere.

A. 韩国
- South Korea.

B. 日本
- Japan.

C. 越南
- Vietnam.

D. 印度
- India.

4 查阅资料，日本在下面哪些方面受到了唐朝文化的影响？［多选］（　　）

Search the information and find out the aspects that Japan had been influenced by culture in Tang Dynasty. (Multiple Answer Question)

A. 建筑
- Architecture.

B. 饮食
- Diet.

C. 文字
- Characters.

D. 中医中药
- Traditional Chinese medicine.

小 结 Summary

通过这些交往，我们也能看到，文化不是一成不变的，也不是僵化的。中国文化其实是在不断吸纳与传播中丰富起来的，无论是官方还是民间，一直都在对外交往中拓展着自己的视野，并不断融合发展。

All the exchanges tell us that culture is not static or rigid. Chinese culture is a beneficiary of continuous absorption and dissemination as it has been expanding its horizons outwards and integrated into its developmet both at official level and in people-to-people sphere.

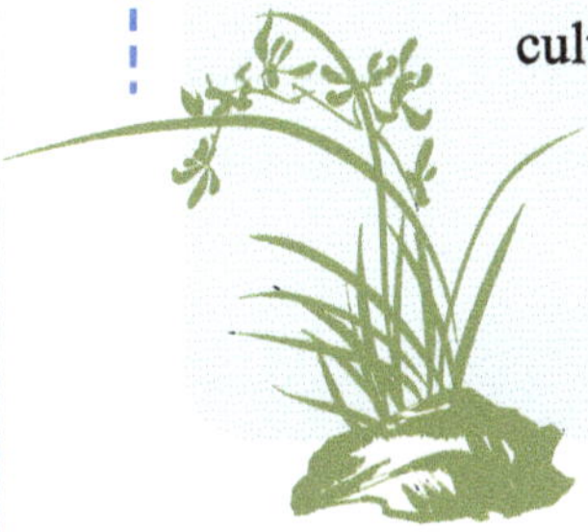

单元结语

CONCLUSION

从个人一日三餐的饮食，到国家庞大机构的治理，再到国与国之间的交流与融合，在中国，个体行为和国家行为之间有着密不可分的关联。深入了解，你才能发现这个古老大国是怎样用“礼”维系起个人、家庭与国家的。

From an individual's three meals a day, to the governance of huge national institutions, and further to the exchanges and communication with other countries, individual behaviors and state behaviors are inextricably linked in China. Only through a deep understanding can you see how this ancient country has used "rites" to hold together individuals, families and the nation.

第四单元 Unit 4

和 Harmony

单元导入 | INTRODUCTION

《论语》里说：“礼之用，和为贵。”意思是说，很多外在形式上的礼仪，最终都是为了达到和谐的目的。这种“和”的思想，扎根在中国人的精神世界，渗透在日常生活的方方面面。

According to *The Analects of Confucius,* “In conducting the rites, harmony is the most important principle.” It means that though etiquette may seemingly extrinsic, its main purpose actually is to create harmony. The idea of “harmony” is rooted in the spiritual world of Chinese people and permeates each and every aspect of life.

13 家和方能万事兴

Harmony Brings Prosperity

热身 Warm-up

每年的一、二月份，中国的交通都会陷入超负荷运行中。在40多天里，20多亿人次，通过汽车、火车或飞机在中国大地上流动。有人说，这是人类历史上规模最大的周期性迁徙。这就是春运，也即春节期间的交通运输。

这么庞大的流动其实只有一个目的——回家过年。“有钱没钱，回家过年”，不管票有多难买，路有多遥远，中国人都会想办法在春节前赶回家过年。春节，就是中国人的新年，这是属于全体家庭成员的重要节日。在中国，除了春节，以团圆为目的的节日还有元宵节和中秋节。

Every year in January or February, transportation in China becomes overloaded. In these forty days, cars, trains, or planes are used more than two billion times as people move about the country. It has been said that this is the largest cyclical migration in human history. This is called "spring travel" – the mass transportation of people that occurs around Spring Festival.

This enormous movement is for one purpose – to go home for Spring Festival, i.e., the Chinese New Year. No matter whether one is rich or poor, no matter how difficult to get a ticket or how long the distance is, Chinese people always find a way to get home before Spring Festival. It is an important festival that belongs to every member of the family. Festivals for the purpose of reunion also include Lantern Festival and Mid-Autumn Festival.

- 想一想，自己国家最重要的节日是什么？有什么特别的庆祝形式吗？
  What is the most important festival in your country? Is there any special form of celebration for it?

13.1 过年的习俗

Customs of Celebrating the New Year

英文课文见P167

春节是中国农历[1]新年的第一天，新年的前一天叫除夕。除夕之夜，全家人一定要聚在一起吃年夜饭，辞旧迎新。这时中国很多地方，尤其是北方人的餐桌上少不了饺子，而南方人则爱吃年糕。从20世纪80年代开始，庆祝春节，除了年夜饭，还有一档称为“春晚”的电视节目。这档跨年的晚会用歌舞、相声[2]、小品[3]、魔术、杂技、戏曲等文艺形式传达着喜庆和团圆的气氛。

春节期间，家家户户都要贴春联、挂年画。人们在红纸上用毛笔写上两句字数相同、意思相对的吉利话，贴在大门的左右两边，这就是春联。春联贴在外面，而走进屋里你又能看到年画。年画与中国画不同，主题明确直接，色彩艳丽夸张。像“老鼠嫁女”，画的是一群吹

吹打打的老鼠抬着花轿，非常热闹地送女儿出嫁，谁知却把女儿送到了猫的家里。老鼠们都被猫吃掉，是辛勤的劳动者朴素的心愿。

春节最常见的习俗是逛庙会。庙会起源于宗教祭祀活动，后来逐渐成为娱乐性的集会。各地庙会风格不同，但其中一定会有花样繁多的表演、美味可口的小吃和丰富多彩的工艺品，因此成为过年中最热闹的习俗。

注释 Notes

① 农历：中国现行的传统历法，是一种阴阳合历，与二十四节气相对应，适用于农业生产。

Lunar calendar: At present, traditional Chinese calendar is a combination of *yin* and *yang*, which corresponds to the 24 solar terms and is applied to agricultural production.

② 相声：一种民间说唱曲艺，以说、学、逗、唱为特点。

Crosstalk: It is a folk art of talking and singing. It highlights its characteristics in the form of talking, imitating, amusing and singing.

③ 小品：通过形体和语言表演一个比较简单的场景。

Opusculum: It performs a relatively simple scene through body and language.

生词 Words and expressions

1	辞旧迎新	cíjiù-yíngxīn	to ring out the old year and ring in the new year
2	档	dàng	a measure word for programs
3	传达	chuándá	to convey; to transmit

4	团圆	tuányuán	reunion
5	艳丽	yànlì	bright-colored and beautiful
6	出嫁	chūjià	(of a woman) to get married
7	辛勤	xīnqín	industrious; hard-working
8	朴实	pǔshí	simple; plain
9	集会	jíhuì	assembly
10	繁多	fánduō	a rich variety of

练习 Exercises

1 阅读课文，下面哪个是过年中最热闹的活动？（　　）

Read the text and find out the liveliest event during the Chinese New Year.

A. 吃年夜饭

- Having New Year's Eve dinner.

B. 贴春联、挂年画

- Pasting Spring Festival couplets and hanging New Year pictures.

C. 看"春晚"

- Watching Spring Festival Gala.

D. 逛庙会

- Visiting the temple fair.

2 欣赏下面几幅作品，请问哪幅是中国传统的年画？（　　）

Enjoy the following works and find out the traditional Chinese New Year picture.

A.

B.

C.

D.

③ 阅读课文，下列哪项与庙会无关？（　　）

Read the text and find out the one that is not related to the temple fair.

A. 美味可口的小吃

■ Delicious snacks.

B. 凄美动人的爱情故事

■ A poignant love story.

C. 丰富多彩的工艺品

■ Various crafts.

D. 花样繁多的表演

■ Multifarious performances.

4 阅读课文，下面哪种食物是春节的传统食物？［多选］（　　）

Read the text and find out the traditional food for Spring Festival. (Multiple Answer Question)

A.

B.

C.

D.

5 思考题：你们国家过年吗？过年的时候有什么特殊的食物和民俗活动呢？

Does your country celebrate the New Year? What special food and folk activities during the New Year?

13.2 元宵与花灯

Yuanxiao and Larnterns

英文课文见P168

从农历正月初一到十五都是“过年”，正月十五这天是元宵节，这一天既是“过年”的最后一天，也是一年中第一个有圆月的日子。元宵节的习俗是吃元宵。这种圆圆的食物在南方也称为汤圆，虽然做法上与元宵有些不同，但都是光滑的表皮里裹着各种好吃的馅儿。无论是元宵还是汤圆，名字里都透着“团圆”的寓意。

元宵节最主要的庆祝形式是赏花灯。在元宵灯会上，各种形态的彩灯把节日的夜晚装点得分外美丽。这时，如果你看到灯下有人仰着脖子，那可能是在猜灯谜。灯谜是挂在彩灯上的谜语，一边赏灯，一边猜谜，很有趣味。实际上，古代元宵节设置灯谜灯会，有着特殊而美好的期待。宋代词人欧阳修的词里说：“去年元夜时，花市灯如昼。月上柳梢头，人约黄昏后。”[①]显然，在古代，元宵节就像是传统的情人节，是有缘人相遇的日子。

注释 Note

① "去年元夜时，花市灯如昼。月上柳梢头，人约黄昏后。"：出自《生查子·元夕》，是宋代文学家欧阳修的词作。这几句词描写的是两个在灯会上相遇的年轻人互生好感，从而约定再次相见的情节。

"Last year on lunar festive night, larnterns mid blooms shone as daylight. When the moon rose atop willow trees, my lover had a tryst with me.": It is from *Sheng Chazi·Yuan Xi*, a poem by Ouyang Xiu, a litterateur of the Song Dynasty. It describes a scene of two young people, who met at Lantern Festival and had a good impression on each other, made an appointment to meet again.

生词 Words and expressions

1	正月	zhēngyuè	the first lunar month
2	初	chū	at the beginning of
3	裹	guǒ	to wrap
4	馅儿	xiànr	filling; stuffing
5	透	tòu	with; through
6	寓意	yùyì	implied meaning
7	装点	zhuāngdiǎn	to decorate
8	分外	fènwài	particularly; especially
9	仰	yǎng	to face upward
10	谜语	míyǔ	riddle
11	设置	shèzhì	to set up

12	显然	xiǎnrán	obvious
13	有缘	yǒuyuán	destined

练习 Exercises

1 阅读课文，元宵节的传统食物是什么？［多选］（　　）

Read the text and find out the traditional food for Lantern Festival. (Multiple Answer Question)

A. 汤圆
- *Tangyuan*.

B. 团圆
- Reunion.

C. 元宵
- *Yuanxiao*.

D. 年糕
- New Year cakes.

2 阅读课文，关于元宵节，哪种描述是不正确的？（　　）

Read the text and find out the wrong description about Lantern Festival.

A. 元宵节是“过年”的最后一天
- Lantern Festival is the last day of the celebration of the "New Year".

B. 元宵和汤圆这两个名字都有“团圆”的寓意
- Both the names *yuanxiao* and *tangyuan* are imbued with the meaning of "reunion".

C. 元宵节是中国的情人节
- Lantern Festival is Chinese Valentine's Day.

D. 古代设置的赏花灯、猜灯谜也是为了帮助有缘人相遇
- In ancient times, lanterns and riddles were set up to help people meet each other.

3 如果你在元宵节的灯会上读到以下灯谜，你能猜出来吗？

If you read the following lantern riddles during Lantern Festival, can you guess them?

1）脱下红黄衣，七八个兄弟，紧紧抱一起，酸甜各有味，大家都喜欢。（打一水果）

After taking off the red and yellow clothes, the seven or eight brothers hug each other tightly with sour and sweet tastes. Everyone likes them. (The riddle is about a fruit.)

2）麻壳子，红里子，里面裹着白胖子。（打一农作物）
In the hemp shell and red lining wrapped white fat men. (The riddle is about a crop.)

3）耳朵长，尾巴短。只吃菜，不吃饭。（打一动物）
It has long ears and a short tail. It eats only vegetables, not meals. (The riddle is about an animal.)

4）一个小姑娘，生在水中央，身穿粉红衫，坐在绿船上。（打一种花）
A little girl, born in the middle of the water, wears in pink and sits in a green boat. (The riddle is about a flower)

13.3 中秋与团圆

Mid-Autumn Festival and Reunion

英文课文见P168

每年农历八月十五是中秋节，顾名思义，这一天正好在秋天的中间，天气凉爽舒适。这天晚上的月亮又圆又亮，象征着团圆，是远方的孩子回家与父母团聚的日子。同时，古人认为月亮的运行与庄稼收成有很大关系，因此在八月十五这天形成了拜月、祭月的习

《嫦娥奔月》 任率英绘

Chang'e Flying to the Moon
drawn by Ren Shuaiying

俗，嫦娥奔月[①]、玉兔捣药[②]这样与月亮有关的民间传说流传至今。更有无数诗人写出了大量借月亮寄托相思的诗句，比如“举头望明月，低头思故乡”（李白《静夜思》[③]），“海上生明月，天涯共此时”（张九龄《望月怀远》[④]）。

中秋节流传至今最主要的节日食物是月饼。把包着馅儿的面团压成扁圆形，烤熟后就成了金黄色的月饼。吃月饼的时候，真像是把天上的圆月也捧在了手心里。圆圆的月饼所传达的自然也是“团圆”的寓意。

注释 Notes

① 嫦娥奔月：中国上古时期的神话传说，故事里嫦娥吃下了西王母赐给丈夫的不死之药，飞到了月宫。“嫦娥奔月”的神话源自古人对月亮的崇拜。

Chang'e flying to the moon: It is an ancient Chinese myth. It tells the story of Chang'e who was forced to take an immortal medicine given to her husband by Queen Mother and flew to the moon palace. It is originated from the ancients' worship of the moon.

② 玉兔捣药：中国神话传说，相传月亮中有一只兔子，浑身洁白如玉，所以称作“玉兔”。玉兔用玉杵不停地捣药，服用这种药丸的人可以成仙。久而久之，玉兔便成为月亮的代名词。

Jade Rabbit pounding herbs: It is a Chinese myth. It is said that there is a rabbit in the moon. Being as white as jade, it is called "Jade Rabbit". Jade Rabbit holds the jade pestle and pounds the medicine constantly all the time. Taking these pills, a person can become an immortal being. As time passes, Jade Rabbit becomes a synonym of the moon.

③《静夜思》：唐代诗人李白所作的一首五言古诗，诗句描写了秋日夜晚诗人在屋内抬头望月的感受，表达了客居思乡之情。

Thoughts on a Tranquil Night: It is a five-character poem written by Li Bai, a poet in Tang Dynasty. The poem describes his homesickness by looking up at the moon in the house on an autumn night.

④《望月怀远》：唐代诗人张九龄的作品。这首诗是望月怀思的名篇，表达了对远方亲人的思念之情。

Looking at the Moon and Longing for One Far away: It is written by Zhang Jiuling, a poet in Tang Dynasty. It is a masterpiece of nostalgia and expresses his longing for relatives far away.

生词 Words and expressions

1	顾名思义	gùmíng-sīyì	just as its name implies
2	庄稼	zhuāngjia	crops
3	祭月	jì yuè	to offer oblations for the moon
4	寄托	jìtuō	to place (hope, etc.) on
5	面团	miàntuán	paste

练习 Exercises

1 阅读第十三课的课文，判断下面的表达是否正确。

Read Lesson 13 and tell whether the following statements are true or false.

1）春节第一天的晚上，全家人要在一起吃年夜饭。（　）

- On the evening of the first day of Spring Festival, the whole family will have a New Year's Eve dinner together.

2）关于春节的传统食物，北方是饺子，南方是年糕。（　）

- The traditional food of Spring Festival is *jiaozi* (dumplings) in north China and *niangao* (New Year cakes) in south China.

3）年画比中国画主题更明确、色彩更艳丽。（　）

- New Year pictures have a clearer theme and brighter colors than Chinese paintings.

4）元宵和汤圆的名字都有“团圆”的寓意。（　）

- Both *yuanxiao* and *tangyuan* have the meaning of "reunion".

5）元宵节最主要的庆祝形式是猜灯谜。　（　　）

■ The primary way to celebrate Lantern Festival is to guess lantern riddles.

6）中秋节赏月来自于祭月，借月亮寄托思念。　（　　）

■ Enjoying the full moon in the Mid-Autumn Festival is originated from offering sacrifices to the moon, and it also expresses people's sentiment of missing.

2 阅读课文，以下哪种是中秋节的传统食物？（　　）

Read the text and find out the traditional food for Mid-Autumn Festival.

A.

B.

C.

D.

3 阅读课文，以下哪些食物的名字包含“团圆”的寓意？［多选］（　　）

Read the text and find out the food implying reunion. (Multiple Answer Question)

A. 汤圆

■ *Tangyuan.*

B. 元宵

■ *Yuanxiao.*

C. 月饼

■ Moon cakes.

D. 饺子

■ *Jiaozi.*

E. 年糕

■ New Year cakes.

4 思考题：说说自己国家有哪些重要的节日？这些节日里有哪些节日美食？它们有什么么样的寓意？

What festivals are celebrated in your country? What foods are offered for those festivals and what are their implied meanings?

小结 Summary

事实上，在这些传统节日里，无论是好吃的还是好玩儿的，都只是为了传达节日的欢快气氛，而把家人团聚在一起，才是过节最主要的目的。中国人认为，家庭的团圆和睦会带来个人事业的发展和整个社会的安定，也就是“家和万事兴”。而从节日里反映出来的家庭观，则来源于长久以来主导中国的儒家思想。

In fact, these tasty or exciting parts of traditional Chinese festivals are only to create a pleasant atmosphere; to bring the family together is the main purpose of festivals. Chinese people believe that family togetherness and reunion will benefit individual development and social stability, that is, “a family in harmony ever prospers.” And the family values reflected in these festivals were originated from Confucianism, the dominant philosophy of China for a long time.

14 君子求和不求同

Harmony in Diversity

热身 Warm-up

当你在中国西南腹地的大足石刻看到佛祖释迦牟尼两边的坐像时，千万不要惊讶——孔子、老子和释迦牟尼已经在这里和睦相处了900多年。

When visiting the Dazu Rock Carvings in the hinterlands of southwest China, you will see two statues seated beside Sakyamuni (Gautama Buddha), the patriarch of Buddhism, and please do not be suprised – Confucius, Laozi, and Sakyamuni have been sitting here in harmony for more than nine centuries.

- 想一想，自己国家有哪些智者，他们说过什么样的名言？对你有什么启发？
  Which wise men in your country, and what are their famous sayings? What inspirations can you get?

14.1 儒家思想与孔孟

Confucianism and Confucius and Mencius

英文课文见P169

儒家不是一个宗教，称它为学派更合适，孔子[①]则是这个学派的创始人。孔子生活在公元前500多年的春秋时期，当时中国有许多诸侯国，统治者们都希望能找到帮助自己治理国家的人。最初，孔子在各国间周游，希望能得到君主的任用，从而施行自己的政治主张。后来他发现，在当时的社会，他的政治理想很难实现。于是孔子回到家乡，广收门徒，希望把自己的思想传播出去。传说孔子有三千学生，其中比较出众的有七十二人，后人把孔子和他弟子的言论和思想放进了一本叫《论语》的小书里。这本小书对中国人的思想产生了巨大的影响。

孔子最核心的思想是“仁”与“礼”。仁的核心是爱人，并强调每个人都要学会换位思考，“己所不欲，勿施于人”，自己不想做的事情也不要强求他人。而“礼”的最终目的是调整人与人之间的关系，使人际关系变得更加和谐，也就是“礼之用，和为贵”。

儒家思想形成过程中的另一个重要人物是孟子②。孟子比孔子晚了一个世纪，但他的人生故事与孔子非常相似。孟子的口才很好，他也在各国奔走，试图说服统治者用严格的道德来约束自己，并希望他们关爱人民，发展生产。然而孟子的主张也没有得到统治者的重视。孟子的思想被记录在《孟子》一书中而得到流传。

实际上，孔子和孟子生活在中国历史上一个重要的思想启蒙时代，社会发生巨大变革，不同学派同时存在，相互之间展开激烈的论辩和竞争。儒家学说只是当时众多思想中的一种。但一百多年后，儒家思想得到汉代最高统治者的青睐，逐渐成为中国的思想正统。历代王朝不断巩固这种传统，并把儒家的经典著作作为科举考试的指定教材。由此，儒家思想对中国人的价值观念、思维方式和民族性格产生了深远的影响。2000多年来，中国人始终按照儒家思想所提倡的那样，做人做事力求把握分寸，遵守规矩，追求中庸。

注释 Notes

① 孔子（前551—前479）：名丘，字仲尼，春秋时期思想家、政治家、教育家，儒家学派创始人。

Confucius (551 BC– 479 BC): Confucius was known as Kong Qiu or Kong Zhongni. He is a ideologist, statesman, educator, and the founder of Confucianism in the Spring and Autumn Period.

② 孟子（约前372—前289）：名轲，字子舆，战国时期思想家、政治家、教育家，儒家学派的代表人物，与孔子并称"孔孟"。

Mencius (around 372 BC–289 BC): Mencius was known as Meng Ke or Meng Ziyu. He is a ideologist, statesman, educator in the Warring States Period. He is a representative of Confucianism. Confucius and Mencius are collectively known as "Kong-Meng".

生词 Words and expressions

1	儒家	Rújiā	Confucianist
2	学派	xuépài	school of thought
3	创始人	chuàngshǐrén	founder
4	周游	zhōuyóu	to travel round
5	君主	jūnzhǔ	monarch; sovereign
6	任用	rènyòng	to appoint; to give one a post
7	主张	zhǔzhāng	proposal; opinion
8	门徒	méntú	disciple; follower
9	核心	héxīn	core

10	仁	rén	benevolence
11	礼	lǐ	the proprieties; etiquette
12	换位	huànwèi	transposition
13	调整	tiáozhěng	to adjust
14	口才	kǒucái	eloquence
15	奔走	bēnzǒu	to be busy running about
16	试图	shìtú	to attempt; to try
17	说服	shuōfú	to persuade; to convince
18	约束	yuēshù	constraint; restraint
19	启蒙	qǐméng	enlightenment
20	论辩	lùnbiàn	debate
21	青睐	qīnglài	favour
22	正统	zhèngtǒng	orthodox
23	巩固	gǒnggù	to consolidate; to solidify
24	分寸	fēncun	proper limits for speech or action; sense of propriety
25	中庸	zhōngyōng	golden mean; moderation

练习 Exercises

1 阅读课文，儒家学派的创始人是谁？（　　）

Read the text and find out the founder of Confucianism.

A. 老子
- Laozi.

B. 孟子
- Mencius.

C. 孙子
- Sunzi.

D. 孔子
- Confucius.

2 阅读课文，下面哪一项不是儒家学派的思想？（ ）

Read the text and find out the one that is not a Confucian thought.

A. 己所不欲，勿施于人
- Do not impose on others what you yourself do not desire.

B. 追求中庸
- Pursue the golden mean.

C. 清静无为
- Be quiet and let things take their own courses.

D. 要学会换位思考和善待别人
- Learn to empathize and treat others well.

3 阅读课文，儒家思想在哪个朝代成为中国的思想正统？（ ）

Read the text and find out when Confucianism became the orthodox thought in China.

A. 春秋时期
- Spring and Autumn Period.

B. 战国时期
- Warring States Period.

C. 秦朝
- Qin Dynasty.

D. 汉朝
- Han Dynasty.

4 阅读课文，下面哪项是中国人的处事原则？［多选］（ ）

Read the text and find out which of the following are Chinese principles of doing things. (Multiple Answer Question)

A. 遵守规矩
- Follow the rules.

B. 追求中庸
- Pursue the golden mean.

C. 做人做事把握分寸
- Hold a sense of propriety.

D. 以和为贵

■ Harmony is the most precious.

5 查阅资料，看看下面这些来自《论语》里的句子都是什么意思。

Search the information and find out the meaning of the following sentences in *The Analects of Confucius.*

1）不在其位，不谋其政。

2）君子坦荡荡，小人长戚戚。

3）父母在，不远游，游必有方。

4）言必信，行必果。

14.2 道家思想与老子

Taoism and Laozi

英文课文见P170

宇宙大爆炸假说①认为，宇宙由一个密度极大、温度极高的初始状态开始，经过不断的膨胀逐渐演化成今天的形态。中国道家思想的创始人老子②在2000多年前阐述了一个类似的观点。在他看来，宇宙的起源是虚无，万物都是按一生二、二生三的演进顺序逐渐形成的。

看到这里也许你已经发现，比起孔子，老子更像一位哲学家，思考的是天地万物运行的规律。这个规律被老子称为“道”。老子认为，“道”没有形状，看不见也摸不着，然而又无处不在，蕴含在一切事物当中。这种对事物本质的认识和解释是道家理论的基础。按照这个规律，老子提出，万物（包括人在内）都应该顺应规律，不要用自己的意志去干预。这种态度就像水流经过的地方自然会形成水沟一样，是很自然的事情。

老子所说的“道”既看不见，也无法描述，因此道家思想总带有一些神秘色彩。借助这种神秘色彩，一种宗教在东汉时期渐渐形成，这就是道教。道教是中国本土发展起来的宗教，有一套完整而庞大的人物谱系，称为神仙。历史上，道教在中国民间有很强的吸引力，它告诉人们，通过长期的修炼可以成为长生不老的神仙，也就是中国民间常说的“得道成仙”。

道家思想对中国人的审美有很大的影响，中国人在艺术创作中追求的形神关系、虚实关系等都来源于道家思想。而道教在民间的发展则造就了中国有名的道教圣地——武当山，武当功夫是中国功夫的一个重要流派。

《老子骑牛图》 明 张路

Picture of Laozi Riding a Bull
drawn by Zhang Lu of Ming Dynasty

注释 Notes

① 大爆炸假说：现代宇宙学中最有影响力的一种学说。它的主要观点是认为宇宙曾有一段从热到冷的演化史。在这个时期里，宇宙体系在不断地膨胀，使物质

密度从密到疏地演化，如同一次规模巨大的爆炸。

The Big Bang hypothesis: It is the most influential theory in modern cosmology. Its main point is that the universe had a history of evolution from hot to cold. During this period, the cosmic system is constantly expanding, causing the density of matter to evolve from dense to sparse, like a huge explosion.

② 老子：姓李，名耳，字聃，春秋末期人，中国古代思想家，道家学派创始人。

Laozi: Known as Li Er or Li Dan and born in the late Spring and Autumn Period, Laozi is an ideologist in ancient China. He is the founder of Taoism.

生词 Words and expressions

1	爆炸	bàozhà	to explode
2	假说	jiǎshuō	hypothesis
3	密度	mìdù	density
4	膨胀	péngzhàng	to expand
5	演化	yǎnhuà	to evolute
6	阐述	chǎnshù	to state
7	虚无	xūwú	nothingness; nihility
8	万物	wànwù	all things on the earth
9	演进	yǎnjìn	evolution
10	哲学	zhéxué	philosophy
11	无处不在	wúchù-búzài	everywhere; anywhere
12	蕴含	yùnhán	to contain; to imply

13	顺应	shùnyìng	to comply with; to conform to
14	意志	yìzhì	will; volition
15	干预	gānyù	to intervene
16	神秘	shénmì	mysterious; mystical
17	谱系	pǔxì	pedigree; ancestry
18	吸引力	xīyǐnlì	attraction
19	神仙	shénxiān	immortal being
20	修炼	xiūliàn	(of Taoists) to try to make pills of immortality and cultivate vital energy
21	得道成仙	dédào-chéngxiān	to be immortal
22	审美	shěnměi	appreciation of beauty
23	造就	zàojiù	to give rise to
24	流派	liúpài	school

练习 Exercises

1 阅读课文，下面哪句话体现了道家理论的基础？（　　）

Read the text and find out the sentence that reflects the foundation of Taoism.

A. 宇宙的起源是虚无
- The origin of the universe is nothingness.

B. “道”无形，但又无处不在，蕴含在一切事物当中
- "Tao" is invisible and ubiquitous. It is contained in everything.

C. 人通过长期的修炼可以成为长生不老的神仙
- People can become immortal beings through long-term cultivation.

D. “道”既看不见，也无法描述
- "Tao" can neither be seen nor described.

2 阅读课文，如果想感受道教文化，可以去哪个地方？（　　）

Read the text and find out the place to go to if you want to experience Taoist culture.

A. 泰山
- Mount Tai.

B. 黄山
- Mount Huang.

C. 武当山
- Mount Wudang.

D. 五台山
- Mount Wutai.

3 阅读课文，关于道家哪种描述是不正确的？（　　）

Read the text and find out the wrong description about Taoism.

A. 道家思想的创始人是老子
- The founder of Taoism is Laozi.

B. 道家思考的是天地万物运行的规律
- Taoists think about the laws of the universe.

C. 万物，包括人在内，都应该顺应规律，不要用自己的意志去干预
- All things, including people, should follow the law, and should not use their own will to interfere.

D. 受道家和儒家思想的影响，道教是中国本土发展起来的宗教
- Influenced by Taoism and Confucianism, Taoism is a religion developed in China

4 阅读课文，以下哪项体现了道家思想对中国人的影响？［多选］（　　）

Read the text and find out the ones that reflect the influence of Taoism on Chinese people. (Multiple Answer Question)

A. 关爱他人，换位思考
- Take a transpositional consideration for others.

B. 把生命看得十分重要
- Life is very important.

C. 中国民间认为通过长期修炼可以“得道成仙”
- Chinese people believe that through long-term cultivation, one can be immortal.

D. 中国人在艺术创作中追求的形神关系、虚实关系
- Chinese people pursue the relationship between form and spirit and that between reality and form in artistic creation.

5 查阅资料，辨认以下哪些是儒家思想，哪些是道家思想，并连线。
Search the information, sort the following thoughts into Confucianism or Taoism and match them.

儒家思想 Confucianism	克己复礼为仁 Self-abnegation is benevolence.
道家思想 Taoism	道可道，非常道 Tao that can be described is not universal and eternal Tao.
	仁者见仁，智者见智 The benevolent see benevolence and the wise see wisdom.
	天地之道，极则反，盈则损 The way of the heaven and the earth, the extreme will lead to the opposite and too much profit will incur loss.
	非礼勿视，非礼勿听 See no evil and hear no evil.

14.3 佛教的融入

The Assimilation of Buddhism

英文课文见P171

佛教起源于古印度，大约在汉朝时传入中国。随着丝绸之路的繁荣，河西走廊[①]上的敦煌莫高窟逐渐形成了一座佛教艺术宝库。在这里，你既能读到精美壁画里的佛经故事，也能欣赏到大至30多米、小至几厘米的精美佛像。如果把莫高窟里的所有艺术品一一排列，你会发现自己进入了一座25千米长的艺术长廊。

从敦煌向南，来到西南的四川，你能见到世界上最高的石刻佛像——乐山大佛。这座佛像完全在峭壁上开凿出来，高达71米，用了90年才完成。欣赏乐山大佛，只靠眼睛是不够的。你可以顺着山上的栈道来到佛像底部，站在可以容下100多人的大佛脚上。抬头仰视，佛就是山，山就是佛。

类似莫高窟和乐山大佛这样的佛教建筑，在中国还有很多，更不用提遍及各地的寺庙。很多中国人信佛，会到寺庙里上香许愿，但削去头发做和尚或尼姑的却并不多。中国人更多地受到儒家思想的影响，比较务实，更关注生活本身。而作为一种外来的宗教，佛教与儒家、道家思想经历了多次碰撞后，逐渐走向融合，它们一起影响着中国人的精神世界。中国历史上，求取功名的读书人如果在现实中遇到挫折，常常会造访深山里的古寺，与高僧交谈，寻求解脱；或者回归乡野，像道家隐士一样过着宁静朴素的生活。

注释 Note

① 河西走廊：中国西部地区的一条狭长地带，因形似走廊且地处甘肃黄河以西而得名。河西走廊在古代是沟通中原与西域的交通要道。

Hexi Corridor: It is a narrow strip of land in western China, named for its resemblance to a corridor and location west of the Yellow River in Gansu Province. In ancient times, Hexi Corridor was the main road connecting the central plains and the Western regions.

生词 Words and expressions

1	宝库	bǎokù	treasure house
2	佛像	fóxiàng	figure of Buddha
3	排列	páiliè	to line up
4	长廊	chángláng	gallery
5	峭壁	qiàobì	cliff
6	栈道	zhàndào	plank road built along the face of a cliff
7	遍及	biànjí	all over
8	许愿	xǔyuàn	to make a wish
9	削	xiāo	to cut
10	和尚	héshang	monk
11	尼姑	nígū	Buddhist nun
12	务实	wùshí	to deal with concrete matters
13	本身	běnshēn	itself

14	碰撞	pèngzhuàng	crash; collision
15	融合	rónghé	to intergrate
16	功名	gōngmíng	scholarly honour or official rank (in feudal times)
17	挫折	cuòzhé	setback
18	造访	zàofǎng	to pay a visit; to call on
19	高僧	gāosēng	eminent monk
20	解脱	jiětuō	to release
21	隐士	yǐnshì	hermit; recluse
22	朴素	pǔsù	simple; plain

练习 Exercises

1 阅读第十四课的课文，判断下面的表达是否正确。
Read Lesson 14 and tell whether the following statements are true or false.

1）孔子的思想被收录在《论语》里，影响了中国1000年。（　）
- Confucius' thought was recorded in *The Analects of Confucius*, which has influenced China for 1,000 years.

2）孔子最核心的思想是"仁"与"礼"。（　）
- The core idea of Confucianism are "benevolence" and "proprieties".

3）孔子和孟子的主张都受到了当时统治者的重视。（　）
- Both the ideas of Confucius and Mencius were valued by the rulers at that time.

4）中国人在艺术创作中追求的形神关系来源于道家思想。（　）
- The relationship between form and spirit by Chinese people in artistic creation originate from Taoism.

5）道家思想崇尚自然，主张顺应规律，不用自己的心意去干预。（　）
- Taoism advocates nature and compliance with laws, and opposes to interfere with your own mind.

6）佛教比较务实，更关注生活本身。（ ）

■ Buddhism is more pragmatic and pays more attention to life itself.

7）敦煌莫高窟和乐山大佛都是佛教建筑。（ ）

■ Both Mogao Caves in Dunhuang and Leshan Giant Buddha are Buddhist architectures.

2 阅读课文，下面哪个画面不会出现在敦煌莫高窟？（ ）

Read the text and find out the picture you cannot see in Mogao Caves.

A.

B.

C.

D.

3 阅读课文，以下哪些人物与佛教有关？［多选］（ ）

Read the text and find out the characters related to Buddhism. (Multiple Answer Question)

A. 玄奘
■ Xuanzang.

B. 鉴真
■ Jianzhen.

C. 孔子
■ Confucius.

D. 老子
■ Laozi.

4 查阅资料，在中国五大宗教中，哪个是唯一发源于中国本土的宗教？（ ）

Search the information and find out the only native one among the five major religions in China.

A. 佛教
- Buddhism.

B. 道教
- Taoism.

C. 天主教
- Catholicism.

D. 伊斯兰教
- Islam.

5 阅读课文，将这几类人和他们可能信奉的思想连线。

Match these types of people with the ideas they might believe in according to the text.

削去头发做和尚的人 People who have their hair cut and become monks	儒家思想 Confucianism
求取功名的读书人 Scholars seeking honor and official rank	道家思想 Taoism
回归乡野，过着宁静朴素生活的人 People who return to the countryside and lead a quiet and simple life	佛教 Buddhism

小结 Summary

儒（儒家）、释（佛教）、道（道家），在中国这片土地上相互包容，和谐相处。这种和谐与“和为贵”的思想不谋而合。

Confucianism, Buddhism, and Taoism all coexist peacefully in China. The harmony coincides with the idea that “harmony and peace are precious”.

15 万物对立且统一

All Things Are Opposite and Unified

热身 Warm-up

看完乐山大佛，你可以再走访一下不远处的道教名山——青城山。这里，随处可见只有黑白两色的太极图。在太极图上，黑白两种颜色像两条首尾交缠在一起的鱼，黑鱼有白眼，白鱼有黑眼。这种性质相反但又相互依存的关系，表达的正是中国最古老的哲学概念——阴阳。

After seeing Leshan Giant Buddha, you can visit the nearby Mount Qingcheng, an important mountain in Taoism. Here, all one can see are black and white *yin-yang* symbols. The black and white on the symbol are like two fish twisted together at the beginning and end, the black fish having a white eye and the white fish having a black eye. They are opposite in nature yet dependent on each other; this relationship expresses China's oldest philosophical concept – *yin* and *yang*.

- 想一想，你怎么理解“对立且统一”的意思？
  How do you understand the meaning of "opposite and unified"?

15.1 阴阳五行

Yin and Yang and the Five Elements

英文课文见P172

除了太极图上的黑和白，在其他事物中你也能看到阴阳，如天和地、太阳和月亮、男性和女性、运动和静止。中国人从这些现象中抽象出“阴阳”的概念，并用它来认识世界。比如，中国人会把看不见太阳的日子称为阴天；把印章上凸出的文字叫作阳文；同一条用来排水的沟，在地面上叫阳沟，在地下叫阴沟。而且，阴阳相互对立，达到极致时就会向对立面转化。比如热代表阳，冷代表阴——最热的夏天过去，天就要凉了；最冷的冬天过去，天就要暖和起来。可以说，阴阳渗透在生活的方方面面，是中国人辩证思想最直接的体现。

五行是中国人观察世界的另一种方式。中国古人把组成世界的基本物质归纳为五种，分别是金、木、水、火、土，称为“五行”。五行之间可以相生，也可以相克。比如水生木，是说水对木能起到有益

的作用；而火克金，则是说火对金有一种破坏作用。与阴阳一样，中国人将五行与生活中的各种现象对应起来，比如方位、数字、颜色、季节等。以方位为例，五行理论认为，水在北方，火在南方，木在东方，金在西方，土在中央。

生词 Words and expressions

1	太极	tàijí	*taiji*
2	印章	yìnzhāng	seal; stamp
3	凸	tū	to bulge
4	对立	duìlì	to oppose; to be antagonistic to

5	极致	jízhì	extreme
6	渗透	shèntòu	to permeate
7	辩证	biànzhèng	dialectical
8	归纳	guīnà	to conclude
9	相生	xiāngshēng	interpromoting relation in the Five Elements
10	相克	xiāngkè	restriction or checking relation in the Five Elements
11	对应	duìyìng	corresponding

练习 Exercises

1 阅读课文，以下哪些事物中渗透着阴阳的思想？［多选］（　　）

Read the text and find out which of the following things are permeated with the theory of *yin-yang*. (Multiple Answer Question)

A.

B.

C.

D.

2 阅读课文，“五行”不包含以下哪种物质？（ ）

Read the text and find out the material not included in the Five Elements.

A.

B.

C.

D.

3 阅读课文，关于五行，哪种描述是不正确的？（ ）

Read the text and find out the wrong description about the Five Elements.

A. 五行是中国人观察世界的一种方式

- The Five Elements is a way for Chinese people to observe the world.

B. 五行之间可以相生，也可以相克

- The Five Elements can beget or restrain each other.

C. 五行中水生木，火克木

- Of the Five Elements, water generates wood and fire overcomes wood.

D. 根据五行与方位的对应关系，水在北方，火在南方。

- According to the correspondence between the Five Elements and the orientation, water is in the north and fire is in the south.

4 请思考，以下哪些说法体现了中国人的辩证思想？［多选］（　　）

Which of the following statements reflect the dialectical thinking of Chinese people? (Multiple Answer Question)

A. 月有阴晴圆缺

- The moon is bright or dim and she may wax and wane.

B. 人有悲欢离合

- People may have sorrows or joys.

C. 风雨之后见彩虹

- We will see the rainbow after the storm.

D. 春暖花开

- Flowers bloom in spring.

15.2 中医和中药

Traditional Chinese Medicine

英文课文见P173

中国的传统医学是建立在阴阳五行理论基础上的。中医认为，人体内运行着阴阳两种“气”，五官和五脏则分别与五行相对应。一旦体内阴阳不平衡，就会引起内在器官的病变，而这些都能反映在外部器官上。比如，中医认为肾脏属水，储藏人体的精气和活力，并与耳朵相通。如果出现耳聋、耳鸣等现象，就可能是肾脏出了问题。所以，中医反对“头痛医头，脚痛医脚”。

中医使用的药物主要有植物、动物和矿物三类，以植物为主，所以也称为“本草”。明代的医学家李时珍，用30多年的时间完成了巨著《本草纲目》，收录了1892种药物和11096个药方，可以看成是中国几千年中药的总结。其中虽然有人参①、鹿茸②、冬虫夏草③这些名贵的中

药材，但大多在日常生活中很常见，比如莲子、菊花、大豆、蜂蜜等。

除了药物，中国人在5000多年前就开始使用一种治疗技术——针灸。中医发现了人体的12条主要经络和8条辅助经络，这些经络就像看不见的通道，串起人体的不同穴位，它们是“气”行走和停留的地方。中医理论认为，在穴位上用手点、用针扎或用药物熏，能使“气”运行顺畅，从而使人体内的阴阳恢复到平衡状态。

注释 Notes

① 人参：属多年生草本植物，其肉质根为强壮滋补药，是名贵中药材。
Ginseng: It is a perennial herb in Araliaceae Panax ginseng. Its fleshy root is a precious Chinese herbal medicine as a strong tonic.

② 鹿茸：梅花鹿或马鹿的雄鹿未骨化而带茸毛的幼角，是名贵中药材。
Pilous antlers: It is the unossified and hairy young horns of the stag of sika deer or red deer. It is a precious Chinese medicinal material.

③ 冬虫夏草：麦角菌科植物冬虫夏草菌寄生在蝙蝠蛾科昆虫幼虫上的子座，它与幼虫的尸体形成的复合体就是冬虫夏草，是名贵中药材。

Cordyceps: It is a precious Chinese herbal medicine. It preys specifically on the larvae of several species of ghost moths.

生词 Words and expressions

1	五官	wǔguān	the five sense organs
2	五脏	wǔzàng	the five internal organs
3	平衡	pínghéng	balance
4	器官	qìguān	organ
5	病变	bìngbiàn	to be diseased
6	肾脏	shènzàng	kidney
7	储藏	chǔcáng	to save and preserve
8	精气	jīngqì	vital essence
9	活力	huólì	vitality
10	聋	lóng	deaf
11	耳鸣	ěrmíng	tinnitus
12	本草	běncǎo	Chinese materia medica
13	巨著	jùzhù	monumental work; masterpiece
14	药方	yàofāng	prescription

15	名贵	míngguì	famous and precious
16	针灸	zhēnjiǔ	acupuncture
17	经络	jīngluò	main and collateral channels
18	辅助	fǔzhù	supplementary
19	穴位	xuéwèi	acupoint
20	熏	xūn	to smoke; to fumigate
21	顺畅	shùnchàng	unhindered; smooth

练习 Exercises

1 阅读课文，以下哪项关于中医的描述是不正确的？（　　）

Read the text and find out the wrong description about traditional Chinese medicine.

A. 中医认为人的体内也运行着阴阳两种“气”

- It is believed in traditional Chinese medicine that human body also runs two kinds of *qi*, namely, *yin* and *yang*.

B. 中医认为五官和五脏分别与五行相对应

- It is believed in traditional Chinese medicine that the five sense organs and the five internal organs correspond to the Five Elements.

C. 中医认为内在器官的病变是由外部器官引起的

- It is believed in traditional Chinese medicine that the lesion of internal organs is caused by the external organs.

D. 中医认为不能“头痛医头，脚痛医脚”

- Traditional Chinese medicine doesn't think it right to treat only the symptoms, not the disease.

2 阅读课文，下面哪些可以用作中药材？［多选］（　　）

Read the text and find out the materials that can be used as traditional Chinese medicine. (Multiple Answer Question)

A.

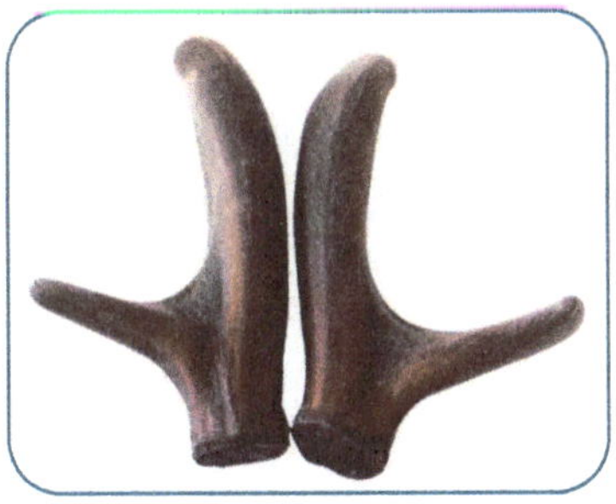

B.

C.

D.

3 阅读课文，如果出现耳聋、耳鸣，中医认为可能是身体哪里出了问题？（　　）
Read the text and find out which part of body is deafness or tinnitus attributed to in Chinese medicine.

A. 心脏
- Heart.

B. 肝脏
- Liver.

C. 肾脏
- Kidney.

D. 脾脏
- Spleen.

4 阅读课文，以下关于《本草纲目》的描述哪项是不正确的？（　　）
Read the text and find out the wrong description about *Compendium of Materia Medica*.

A. 作者是明代著名医学家李时珍
- The author is Li Shizhen, a famous medical scientist in Ming Dynasty.

B. 是中国几千年中医药的总结
- It is a summary of traditional Chinese medicine for thousands of years.

C. 是中国第一部完整的医药学著作

- It is the first complete medical book in China.

D. 书中收录的药材中既有名贵的中药材，又有日常可见的药材

- The medicinal materials in the book include both valuable Chinese herbal medicine and common medicinal materials.

5 查阅资料，辨别下列哪个方法为针灸治疗。［多选］（　　）

Search the information and find out the acupuncture treatment from the following pictures. (Multiple Answer Question)

A.

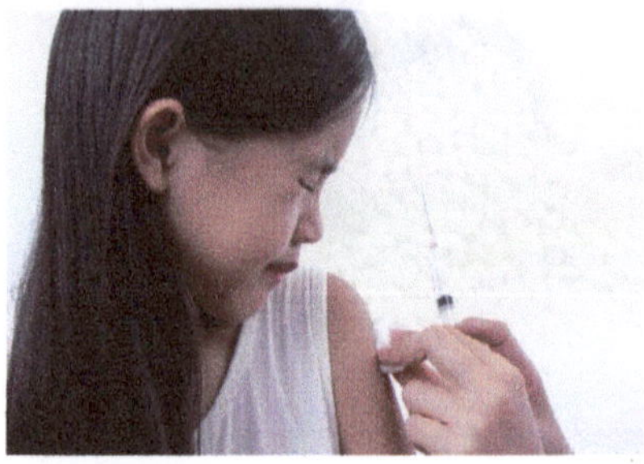

B.

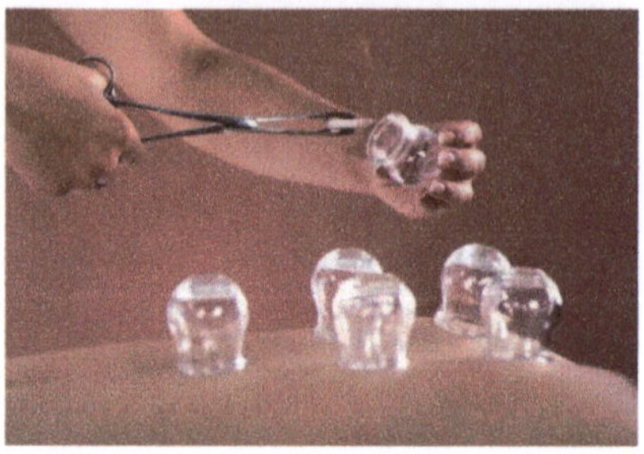

C.

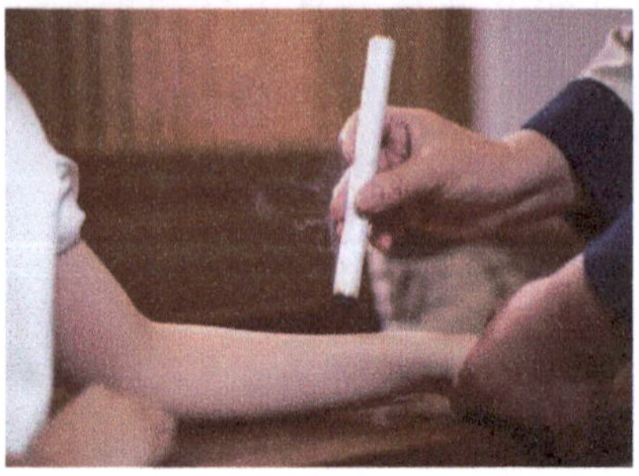

D.

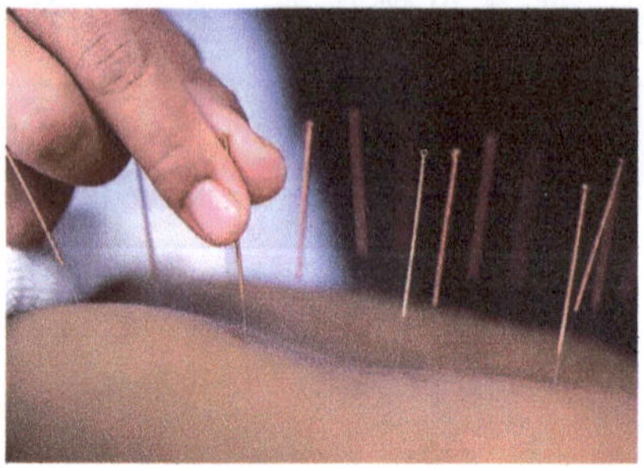

15.3 太极拳与中国功夫

Taijiquan and Chinese Kung Fu

英文课文见P173

除了中医，阴阳理论也与中国人独特的锻炼方式——太极拳有密切

的联系。太极拳在中国民间很流行，既是武术爱好者的首选，也是普通人健身的常见形式。

现在流行的太极拳，一般认为是起源于400年前河南陈家沟的陈氏太极拳，后来分化出了许多不同的流派。但无论哪种流派，太极拳的锻炼目的是一致的，通过柔和的节奏来调节呼吸和肢体，并最终达到阴阳平衡的目的。舒展的动作配合缓慢而均匀的呼吸，使得太极拳具有一定的观赏性。在中国某些重大的节庆场合，常常能看到数千人甚至上万人的太极拳表演。

我们虽然可以把太极拳看成中国功夫的代表，但中国功夫的种类其实要丰富得多。功夫明星李小龙[①]，从小练习的功夫就包括太极拳、咏春拳、螳螂拳等。同时，功夫与武术不同，功夫不仅包括外在的武术，还包括调整气息的气功，也就是俗话说的“外练筋骨皮，内练一口气”。当我们感叹少林武术无坚不摧时，不能忽略他们面壁十

年的修炼。所以，功夫实际上融合了儒家的中和②、道家的守静③和佛家的禅定④思想。从某种意义上讲，中国功夫是中国传统思想的外在体现。

注释 Notes

① 李小龙（1940—1973）：功夫片的开创者，截拳道创始人，著名华人武打电影演员。

Bruce Lee (1940–1973): He is the pioneer of kung fu movies, the founder of Jeet Kune Do, and a famous Chinese martial arts film actor.

② 中和：在《礼记·中庸》中，中和指相对的事物互相抵消，失去各自的性质。

Zhonghe: In *The Book of Rites·Golden Mean*, it means that opposites cancel each other out and thus lose their respective properties.

③ 守静：出自《老子》，意思是保持清静，无所企求。

Shoujing: It is from *Laozi*, which means to keep quiet and do nothing.

④ 禅定：佛教用语，禅与定都是指让心专注于某一对象而达到不散乱的状态。

Zen: It is a Buddhist term to describe focusing on a certain object so as to achieve a state of non-disorganization.

生词 Words and expressions

1	太极拳	tàijíquán	*taijiquan*
2	武术	wǔshù	martial arts
3	首选	shǒuxuǎn	first choice
4	分化	fēnhuà	differentiation; polarization
5	柔和	róuhé	gentle; soft

6	节奏	jiézòu	rhythm; cadence
7	调节	tiáojié	to adjust
8	肢体	zhītǐ	limbs and trunk
9	舒展	shūzhǎn	to stretch; to extend
10	缓慢	huǎnmàn	slow
11	均匀	jūnyún	even; well-distributed
12	观赏性	guānshǎngxìng	appreciation; enjoyability
13	气息	qìxī	breath
14	气功	qìgōng	a system of deep breathing exercises
15	感叹	gǎntàn	to sigh with feeling
16	无坚不摧	wújiān-bùcuī	to be all-conquering
17	面壁	miànbì	to face the wall and meditate

练习 Exercises

1 阅读课文，练习太极拳的目的是什么？（　　）

Read the text and find out the ultimate goal of practicing *taijiquan*.

A. 保护自己
- To protect yourself.

B. 塑身美体
- To keep fit.

C. 调节肢体平衡度
- To adjust body balance.

D. 使身体达到阴阳平衡
- To achieve *yin-yang* balance.

2 阅读课文，以下哪项关于太极拳的描述是不正确的？（　　）

Read the text and find out the wrong description about *taijiquan*.

A. 太极拳与阴阳理论没有联系

- *Taijiquan* has no connection with the theory of *yin* and *yang*.

B. 太极拳起源于中国

- *Taijiquan* was originated in China.

C. 太极拳具有很强的欣赏性

- *Taijiquan* is for appreciation.

D. 太极拳的流派众多

- There are many schools of *taijiquan*.

3 阅读课文，下面哪项属于中国功夫？［多选］（　　）

Read the text and find out which of the following is kung fu. (Multiple Answer Question)

A. 太极拳

- *Taijiquan*.

B. 空手道

- Karate.

C. 咏春拳

- Wing chun.

D. 螳螂拳

- Mantis boxing.

4 阅读课文，中国功夫没有融合哪种思想？（　　）

Read the text and find out the idea that Chinese kung fu has not incorporated.

A. 道家的守静

- *Shoujing* in Taoism.

B. 佛家的禅定思想

- *Zen* in Buddhism.

C. 儒家的中和

- *Zhonghe* in Confucianism.

D. 法家的法治思想

- The rule of law in Legalism.

15.4 《易经》与八卦

The Book of Changes and the Eight Diagrams

英文课文见P174

我们再来看看与阴阳有关的另一部重要经典——《易经》。商代刻在龟甲和兽骨上的甲骨文是用来占卜的，类似祭祀、婚嫁、出行、征战等大事，都需要事先进行占卜，而《易经》就是这样一部记录卜辞的书。

《易经》的一个重要概念是八卦，它的哲学基础是阴阳。“⚊”这个符号代表阳，“⚋”这个符号代表阴。卦，就是由三个这样的符号排列组合而成的。比如：乾卦“☰”由三阳组成，代表天；坤卦“☷”由三阴组成，代表地。

古人对八卦做出了详细的解释。比如，从乾卦和坤卦中，人们得到启示，一个人要像天不停运行一样保持奋斗，要像地生长万物一样博大宽容。（“天行健，君子以自强不息；地势坤，君子以厚德载物。”）由此，《易经》不但为人们提供了认识世界、理解宇宙的方法，也指导人们修炼自己的德行和思想。就连圣人孔子在晚年读《易经》之后也感叹，要是50岁时能读到这部书，就可以不犯大错误了。

武当山上的太极八卦图

The *taiji bagua* diagram on Wudang Mountain

生词 Words and expressions

1	龟甲	guījiǎ	tortoise shell
2	兽骨	shòugǔ	animal bone
3	卜辞	bǔcí	oracle inscriptions of Shang Dynasty on tortoise shells or animal bones
4	启示	qǐshì	enlightenment
5	奋斗	fèndòu	to strive; to struggle
6	博大	bódà	broad and profound
7	宽容	kuānróng	lenient
8	德行	déxíng	moral integrity

练习 Exercises

1 阅读第十五课的课文，判断下面的表达是否正确。
Read Lesson 15 and tell whether the following statements are true or false.

1）阴阳渗透在生活的方方面面，是中国人辩证思想最直接的体现。 (　　)

■ *Yin* and *yang* are in all aspects of life and are the most direct manifestation of Chinese dialectical thinking.

2）五行包括“金、木、水、火、石”，五行相生相克。 (　　)

■ The Five Elements are metal, wood, water, fire, and stone. They generate and overcome each other.

3）中医使用的药物主要有植物、动物和矿物三类，以动物为主。 (　　)

■ The medicines used in traditional Chinese medicine are plants, animals and minerals, with animals taking the primary part.

4）太极拳的锻炼目的是通过柔和的节奏来调节呼吸和肢体，并最终达到阴阳平衡的目的。（　）

■ *Taijiquan* exercises aim to regulate breathing and limbs through a gentle rhythm, and finally to achieve *yin-yang* balance.

5）中国功夫是中国传统思想的内在体现。（　）

■ Chinese kung fu is the inner embodiment of traditional Chinese thought.

6）《易经》的哲学基础是阴阳。（　）

■ The philosophical basis of *The Book of Changes* is *yin* and *yang*.

2 阅读课文，孔子晚年感叹自己哪本书读晚了？（　）

Read the text and find out which book Confucius said he shoud have read it earlier.

A.《论语》
■ *The Analects of Confucius.*

B.《道德经》
■ *The Tao Te Ching.*

C.《易经》
■ *The Book of Changes.*

D.《本草纲目》
■ *Compendium of Materia Medica.*

3 阅读课文，以下哪项关于《易经》的描述是不正确的？（　）

Read the text and find out the wrong description about *The Book of Changes.*

A.《易经》是一部记录卜辞的书
■ *The Book of Changes* is a book recording divination.

B.《易经》是记录在龟甲和兽骨上的甲骨文
■ *The Book of Changes* are oracle bone inscriptions recorded on tortoise shells and animal bones.

C.《易经》为人们提供了认识世界、理解宇宙的方法
■ *The Book of Changes* provides people with methods to know the world and understand the universe.

D.《易经》指导人们修炼自己的德行和思想
■ *The Book of Changes* guides people to cultivate their own virtues and thoughts.

4 阅读课文，思考下列哪项与阴阳理论有密切的联系。［多选］（　　）

Read the text and find out which of the following is closely related to the theory of *yin-yang*. (Multiple Answer Question)

A. 中医
- Traditional Chinese medicine.

B. 太极拳
- *Taijiquan.*

C. 《易经》
- *The Book of Changes.*

D. 中国功夫
- Chinese kung fu.

小结 Summary

中国有个寓言叫“塞翁失马，焉知非福”。在这个寓言故事里，经过多次反转，告诉大家“福”与“祸”是一对相互转化的概念，既对立又统一。这些辩证思想的存在，使朴实的中国人能够直面生活的酸甜苦辣，乐观而从容地生活。

There is a Chinese fable called “塞翁失马，焉知非福”. It is similar to “bad day at black rock”. In this fable, after many reversals, we are told that fortune and misfortune are a pair of mutually transforming relations, which are both opposite and unified. Such dialectical ideas enable Chinese to live optimistically and calmly in facing both the joys and sorrows in life.

16

民胞物与天人合

The Unity of the Heaven and Human

热身 Warm-up

仔细观察汉字“天”，你会发现它包含着一个“人”字。从“天”字的演变过程我们发现，“天”始终与“人”密不可分。这个汉字本身就传达了一种很有哲学意味的思想——天人合一。

A close look at the character “天” (literally meaning “heaven”) shows that it includes the character “人” (literally meaning “human”). From the evolution of the character “天”, we can see that “heaven” has always been inseparable from “人”. The character “天” itself conveys a philosophical idea – the heaven and human are unified.

- 你觉得“天人合一”是什么意思？在你们自己国家，“天”这个概念有没有什么特别的含义？

  What does “the unity of the heaven and human(天人合一)” mean in your opinion? Is there any special meaning for “heaven” in your country?

16.1 风水与环境

Fengshui and Environment

英文课文见P175

“天人合一”最直接的体现大概就是中国人的风水理论了。那么，什么是风水呢？如果你看过2008年北京奥运会开幕式，一定记得这个创意——29个大脚印烟花沿着北京城的中轴线走向主体育场鸟巢[①]。中轴线是一条南北纵线，北京的西城和东城在左右两边形成完美的对称。这种设计就体现了中国人常说的“风水”。

古时候，中国人在城市布局或修建住宅时，第一步要考察的不是材料，而是建筑所在地的地形、水源、风向、土质、朝向等条件，这些条件综合起来，就可以称为风水。风水从本质上讲，追求的是人与自然的

符合风水理论的浙江兰溪诸葛八卦村

Zhugge Bagua Village in Lanxi, Zhejiang Province built in accordance with *fengshui* theory

和谐。同时，人们相信，好的风水能够带来平安和财富。指导人选择风水宝地的风水师是一门古老的职业，他们会观察四周的事物，用罗盘[②]确定方位，用鲁班尺[③]测量距离，为人们挑选好的地理位置。一般来说，风水宝地的建筑与周围环境往往也是非常协调的。金碧辉煌的故宫、风景优美的颐和园和设计精巧的宏村都可以称为风水宝地。

注释 Notes

① 鸟巢：中国国家体育场，是2008年北京奥运会的主体育场。

The Bird's Nest: It is China National Stadium, which is the main stadium for 2008 Beijing Olympic Games.

② 罗盘：用于探测风水的工具。

Compass: It is a tool for geomantic omen (*fengshui*) detection.

③ 鲁班尺：造房盖屋时所用的测量工具，因相传由春秋时代的鲁班发明而得名。

Luban ruler: It is a measuring tool used when building houses. Legend has it that it is named after Lu Ban since it was invented by Lu Ban in the Spring and Autumn Period.

生词 Words and expressions

1	开幕式	kāimùshì	opening ceremony
2	创意	chuàngyì	creativity
3	脚印	jiǎoyìn	footprint
4	中轴线	zhōngzhóuxiàn	central axis
5	纵线	zòngxiàn	ordinate

6	布局	bùjú	layout
7	地形	dìxíng	terrain; landform
8	水源	shuǐyuán	source of water
9	风向	fēngxiàng	wind direction
10	土质	tǔzhì	soil property
11	朝向	cháoxiàng	orientation
12	风水宝地	fēngshuǐ bǎodì	place with auspicious geomantic omens
13	风水师	fēngshuǐshī	geomancer
14	协调	xiétiáo	well-coordinated
15	金碧辉煌	jīnbì-huīhuáng	splendid and magnificent

练习 Exercises

1 阅读课文，中国古人在城市布局或修建住宅时，首先会考察什么？（　　）

Read the text and find out the first thing ancient Chinese people considered when laying out a city or building a house.

A. 价格
- Price.

B. 材料
- Materials.

C. 风水
- *Fengshui.*

D. 距离
- Distance.

2 阅读课文，以下哪项设计中考虑了“风水”？［多选］（　　）

Read the text and find out the design reflecting *fengshui*. (Multiple Answer Question)

A. 北京城布局
- The layout of Beijing city.

B. 故宫
- The Imperial Palace.

C. 宏村
- Hongcun Village.

D. 颐和园
- The Summer Palace.

3 阅读课文，风水不包含什么？（　　）
Read the text and find out the thing that is not included in *fengshui.*

A. 水源
- Water source.

B. 地形
- Terrain.

C. 土质
- Soil property.

D. 建筑风格
- Architectural style.

4 思考题：想想自己国家在修建住宅时会考察哪些因素？
What will be considered in building a house in your country?

16.2 天坛与祭天
Temple of Heaven and Offering Sacrifices to the Heaven

英文课文见P176

在“天人合一”思想中，除了人与自然的和谐，还包括对天的敬畏。古人认为，天在人的头顶上，人应该按照天的规律来做人做事，否则灾祸就会从天而降。对天的敬畏也约束着古代的统治者。皇帝只有宣称自己是天的儿子，百姓才认可他。新皇帝登基后，都要举行祭天仪式。北京的天坛就是为祭天而修建的。

从故宫出来，往东南方向走，就来到了天坛。天坛面积相当于四个故宫那么大，从北到南也按照中轴线布局。北端的祈年殿是天

坛的标志性建筑，各种旅游宣传资料中都能看到它。祈年殿顶部用蓝色琉璃瓦铺成，远远望去与蓝天和谐地融为一体。南端是圜丘坛。圜丘坛由三个同心圆环绕而成，越往里越高。站在最中间的一块圆形石板上轻轻喊一声，立刻就能听到回音从四面八方传来。每年冬至①，皇帝就在这里祭天。可以想象，祭天仪式上气氛庄严，声音洪亮，回音不断，仿佛天上的神在宣读神谕，让人感到天之伟大、人之渺小。

注释 Note

① 冬至：中国二十四节气之一，时间在每年公历12月21日或22日。冬至这天，太阳直射南回归线，北半球昼最短、夜最长。

Winter Solstice: It is one of China's 24 solar terms. The time is from December 21 or 22 of the Gregorian calendar each year. On Winter Solstice, the sun is directly above the Tropic of Capricorn. The northern hemisphere has the shortest day and longest night.

生词 Words and expressions

1	敬畏	jìngwèi	to hold in awe and veneration
2	灾祸	zāihuò	disaster
3	从天而降	cóngtiān'érjiàng	to drop from the sky; very unexpectedly
4	宣称	xuānchēng	to declare
5	登基	dēngjī	to ascend the throne
6	琉璃瓦	liúliwǎ	glazed tile
7	融为一体	róngwéiyìtǐ	integrated
8	同心圆	tóngxīnyuán	concentric circles
9	环绕	huánrào	to embrace; to surround
10	回音	huíyīn	echo; aftersound
11	四面八方	sìmiàn-bāfāng	all directions
12	洪亮	hóngliàng	loud and clear; resonant
13	神谕	shényù	oracle
14	渺小	miǎoxiǎo	minute; tiny

练习 Exercises

1 阅读课文，观察下面哪张图片是天坛的建筑。（　　）

Read the text and find out the building in Temple of Heaven.

A.

B.

C.

D.

2 阅读课文，古时候天坛的用途是什么？（　　）

Read the text and find out the use of Temple of Heaven in ancient times.

A. 百姓祭天的场所

- It was a place for ordinary people to worship the heaven.

B. 皇帝祭天的场所

- It was a place where emperors worshipped the heaven.

C. 庆祝皇帝登基的场所

- It was a place to celebrate emperors' accession to the throne.

D. 皇帝祭祀祖先的场所

- It was a place where emperors worshipped ancestors.

3 阅读课文，古时候天坛在什么时候举行祭天仪式？（　　）

Read the text and find out when the heaven worship ceremony was held in Temple of Heaven in ancient times.

A. 清明
- Qingming.

B. 冬至
- Winter Solstice.

C. 夏至
- Summer Solstice.

D. 春分
- Equinox.

4 阅读课文，天坛的设计体现了中国人的什么思想？［多选］（　　）

Read the text and find out Chinese people's ideas that were reflected in the design of Temple of Heaven. (Multiple Answer Question)

A. 天人合一
- The unity of the heaven and human.

B. 人与自然和谐相处
- The harmony between man and nature.

C. 人要对上天有所敬畏
- People should be in awe of the heaven.

D. 人就应该按照人类自己的想法来
- People should behave according to the laws of human beings.

16.3 四合院的布局

The Layout of Quadrangle Courtyards

英文课文见P176

如果你坐着三轮车在北京后海边上的胡同[①]里穿行，就会见到胡同两边四四方方的院子，它们是四合院。四合院的形状像汉字里的“口”，方方正正，左右对称。“四”是东西南北四面，“合”是四面合在一起，中间是围起来的院落。现在请回想一下前面讲过的故宫，虽然它金碧辉煌，不也是一座豪华版的四合院吗？

四合院是中国传统民居的重要形式，四面的房屋都有讲究，不能随意使用。家族里的长辈住在北面的正房里，晚辈则住东西两侧的厢房。靠南的房子，挨着大门，在古代一般作为用人的住所或者客房。这样的布局使几代人住在一个完整的空间里，其乐融融，可以充分享受天伦之乐。特别重要的是，虽然是居住的地方，院子却占了很大的比例，在其中种花草，养鱼虫，舒适而惬意，形成一个独立于外却又与自然紧密相连的建筑形态。

家庭和美，人与自然和谐，四合院传达着中国人的生活理想。

注释 Note

① 胡同：北京地区街巷的通称。
Hutong: It is a general term for streets and alleys in Beijing.

生词 Words and expressions

1	穿行	chuānxíng	to pass through
2	方方正正	fāngfāngzhèngzhèng	square
3	院落	yuànluò	courtyard
4	豪华	háohuá	luxury
5	民居	mínjū	civil dwellings
6	长辈	zhǎngbèi	elder; senior
7	正房	zhèngfáng	principal room (in a courtyard, usually facing south)
8	晚辈	wǎnbèi	younger generation; juniors
9	厢房	xiāngfáng	wing-room
10	用人	yòngren	servant
11	客房	kèfáng	guest room
12	天伦之乐	tiānlúnzhīlè	happiness of a family
13	其乐融融	qílè-róngróng	with happiness knowing no bounds
14	惬意	qièyì	pleasant; cozy
15	和美	héměi	harmonious and happy

练习 Exercises

1 阅读课文，以下哪个建筑是四合院？（　　）

Read the text and find out the quadrangle courtyard from the following buildings.

A.

B.

C.

D.

2 阅读课文，四合院的形状像哪个汉字？（　　）

Read the text and find out the Chinese character a quadrangle courtyard resembles.

A. 牛
- Cow.

B. 回
- Times.

C. 口
- Mouth.

D. 四
- Four.

3 阅读课文，在四合院里，长辈的房间一般是什么朝向？（　　）

Read the text and find out the orientation of the elder's room in a quadrangle courtyard.

A. 坐南朝北
- Facing north.

B. 坐东朝西
- Facing west.

C. 坐西朝东
- Facing east.

D. 坐北朝南
- Facing south.

4 阅读课文，关于四合院的描述不正确的是哪一项？（　　）

Read the text and find out the wrong description about a quadrangle courtyard.

A. 四合院方方正正，左右对称

- A quadrangle courtyard is a symmetrical square.

B. 四合院的设计参照了故宫

- The design of a quadrangle courtyard referred to the Imperial Palace.

C. 四合院是中国传统民居的重要形式

- A quadrangle courtyard is an important form of Chinese traditional dwellings.

D. 四合院的设计体现了人与自然和谐相处的思想

- The design of a quadrangle courtyard reflects the idea of harmony between man and nature.

16.4 龙与天人合一

Dragons and the Unity of the Heaven and Human

英文课文见P177

中国人说自己是龙的子孙，但很多人都知道，龙是虚构出来的动

物，它是由许多动物组合而成的：身体像蛇，鳞甲像鱼，角像鹿，爪子像老鹰，嘴边的胡须却又像老虎。作为一种图腾，它出现在各种建筑物上、各种艺术品中。

这个虚构的动物在中国历史上长期作为帝王的代名词而存在。人们认为龙是上天的代言人，它能从最深的海底飞到看不见的高空，喷吐出农作物需要的雨水。在古代农业社会，每当大旱时，人们就到龙王庙①祈求龙王②降雨。如此，从敬畏天到敬畏龙，再进一步敬畏真龙天子——皇帝，人们就逐渐把对自然的敬畏转化成了对人的敬畏。所以，龙在某种意义上可以看成是“天人合一”思想的符号化产物。

将多种动物的特性综合到龙身上，体现出中国古人渴望融合自然万物的理想。这种追求人与自然和谐的理想，你在宏村居民的生活中见到过，在打太极拳的时候体验过，在天坛的圜丘坛上聆听过。

注释 Notes

① 龙王庙：供奉龙王的庙宇，在古代是官府及民众遇旱祈雨的地方。
Longwang Temple: It is a temple dedicated to Longwang (literally meaning "Dragon King"). In ancient times, it was the place where officials and ordinary people prayed for rain during drought.

② 龙王：古代神话传说中在水里统领水族的神，掌管兴云降雨。
Longwang: In Chinese myths, he is the king that rules the water clan and is in charge of forming cloud and rain.

生词 Words and expressions

1	虚构	xūgòu	imaginary

2	鳞甲	línjiǎ	scale and shell (of fish or reptile)
3	爪子	zhuǎzi	talon
3	胡须	húxū	beard; moustache
4	图腾	túténg	totem
5	代言人	dàiyánrén	spokesperson
6	喷吐	pēntǔ	to spurt
7	农作物	nóngzuòwù	crops
8	祈求	qíqiú	to pray
9	降雨	jiàng yǔ	rainfall
10	特性	tèxìng	characteristic
11	聆听	língtīng	to listen (respectfully)

练习 Exercises

1 阅读第十六课课文，判断下面的表达是否正确。
Read Lesson 16 and tell whether the following statements are true or false.

1）中国人在城市布局或修建住宅时，第一步要考察的是材料。 (　　)
▪ In city planning or house building, Chinese people will consider the materials first.

2）风水从本质上讲，追求的是人与自然的和谐。 (　　)
▪ *Fengshui* is essentially the pursuit of harmony between human and nature.

3）天坛体现了皇帝对上天的敬畏之情。 (　　)
▪ Temple of Heaven embodies the emperor's reverence for the heaven.

4）圜丘坛是天坛的标志性建筑。 (　　)
▪ Circular Mound Altar is the landmark architecture of Temple of Heaven.

5）四合院里长辈要住正房，晚辈住厢房。 （ ）

- In a quadrangle courtyard, elders should live in the principal room, and the younger generation in the wing-rooms.

6）四合院的设计体现了中国人的生活理想。 （ ）

- The design of a quadrangle courtyard reflects the Chinese ideal of life.

7）龙在某种意义上可以看成是“天人合一”思想的符号。 （ ）

- Drangon can be regarded as a symbol for the idea of harmony between the heaven and human in some sense.

2 阅读课文，在古代中国人的观念中，龙掌管的是什么？（ ）

Read the text and find out what dragon was in charge of in ancient Chinese people's mind.

A. 火
- Fire.

B. 风
- Wind.

C. 电
- Electricity.

D. 雨
- Rain.

3 阅读课文，以下哪项关于中国龙的描述是不正确的？（ ）

Read the text and find out the wrong description about the Chinese dragon.

A. 中国人认为自己是龙的子孙
- Chinese people think they are descendants of dragon.

B. 在古代中国，龙是帝王的代名词
- In ancient China, dragon was synonymous with emperor.

C. 龙体现出中国古人渴望融合自然万物的理想
- Dragon reflects ancient Chinese people wish to integrate the myriad things with nature.

D. 宏村居民在生活中见到过龙
- The residents of Hongcun Village have seen a dragon in their lives.

4 下列哪些事物体现了中国人与自然和谐相处的理想？［多选］（ ）

Which of the following reflects the Chinese idea of "human beings living in harmony with nature"? (Multiple Answer Question)

A. 宏村
- Hongcun Village.

B. 四合院
- Quadrangle courtyards.

C. 中国龙

■ Chinese dragon.

D. 天坛

■ Temple of Heaven.

E. 故宫

■ The Imperial Palace.

5 思考题：想想自己国家有图腾崇拜吗？这些图腾具有什么象征意义？

Is there totem worship in your country? What are the symbolic meanings of these totems?

小结 Summary

在中国人眼里，天是威严无边的，要敬畏，不可冒犯，冒犯就会有灾难降临。同时，“天”下还有“人”，顺应自然又借助自然，打造出舒适的居住环境，才能有人不断繁衍生息。敬天爱人，民胞物与，这大概体现了“靠天吃饭”的中国人最朴素的自然观。

In the eyes of Chinese people, the heaven is majestic and should be held in awe and veneration. People cannot offend it, or disasters will come with offense. Meanwhile, as people live under the heaven, only by conforming to nature and using nature can we create a comfortable living environment and continue to thrive. Chinese people respect the heaven and love people and things. That probably reflects the most simple view of nature of Chinese people who “depend on the heaven for food”.

单元结语

CONCLUSION

2008年北京奥运会开幕式表演中，展示中国5000年文明的卷轴上波涛翻滚，最终定格成一个汉字——“和”。中国人眼里的“和”，是家庭和睦，是阴阳调和，是天人合一。孔子曾经提醒弟子，要做君子，而不要做小人。因为君子既不攀附他人，也不与他人比较，他做自己，而与其他人和谐相处。（“君子和而不同，小人同而不和。”）当然，这种“和”的理想，不仅体现在人与自然之间、人与人之间，也需要体现在国与国之间。

At the opening ceremony of 2008 Beijing Olympic Games, the great waves rolling in the scrolls of China's 5,000 years of civilization were revealed and summarized to a single character "和" (literally meaning "harmony"). Harmony in the minds of Chinese is in concord in the household, reconciliation of *yin* and *yang*, and the unity of the heaven and human. Confucius has reminded his disciples that one should be virtuous rather than mean. A virtuous person does not cling to others or compare with others. He is himself and lives in harmony with others. (“君子和而不同，小人同而不和。”) The ideal of harmony is reflected not only in the relationship between human and nature and that between human themselves, but also in the relationship between nations.

附录01

课文英文翻译

English Texts

Unit 3 Etiquette

Lesson 9

Food Is the Paramount Necessity of the People

9.1 Chinese Food and Cooking

In the long course of the development of agricultural civilization, Chinese people took their food from land, and different dietary customs developed in different parts of the country. “Sweet in the south, salty in the north, spicy in the east and sour in the west” is a way of summarizing the different tastes of various areas. In fact, Chinese food is so diverse that though one were to eat a different kind of Chinese food each day, a lifetime would not be long enough to finish all of them. There are four major cuisines or eight major cuisines in China. Generally speaking, four major cuisines refer to Sichuan cuisine, Shandong cuisine, Cantonese cuisine, and Huaiyang cuisine. Sichuan cuisine ranks the first and includes dishes such as “kung pao chicken” and “mapo tofu”, which are popular around the world. As many overseas Chinese were originally from Canton (Guangdong), its cuisine is also relatively common all over the world. At present, Chinese food is constantly transforming, and “Northeast cuisine”, “Hunan cuisine” and “Shanghai cuisine” all have unique styles.

The vast variety of Chinese food, when it comes down to cooking, has four main points: selecting ingredients, knife work, heat control, and seasoning. Beijing Roast Duck, a favorite of many, must be prepared from "stuffed ducks" from Beijing area to have the correct flavor – this is what is meant by selecting ingredients. Before cooking, the ingredients must be cut in the appropriate manner (filleted, shredded, sliced, chopped, diced, etc.) and in equal amounts for the best taste – this is knife work. After preparing the ingredients, no matter whether the food is stir-fried or steamed, boiled or pan-fried, stewed or deep-fried, the strength of the fire and the length of time essentially determine the quality of a dish – this is heat control. Seasoning, on the other hand, affects the flavor – for example, hot peppers are indispensable to Sichuan cuisine, while Shanxi cuisine is incomplete without sour vinegar.

9.2 The Dining Table and Chopsticks

You might think that the many varieties of Chinese cuisine discussed here have nothing to do with etiquette, but in fact, ancient Chinese etiquette came directly from food and drink. What people ate reflected their position in life, and the differences were quite strict indeed. Today, these complicated classes and rules have disappeared, but the thoughts related to them still affect the culture of dining.

Before delicious food is brought to the table, seating is an important question. Those of higher position or the elderly are usually seated on the upper seats, facing south from the north, or facing the door. In terms of the order of taking a seat, the elderly and important guests are usually seated first, and the others in the order of age or position, which is called that "there is an order between people of high status and low status, and between the elderly and the young".

After being seated, there are also rules for eating. Here we must discuss Chinese people's distinctive eating utensils – chopsticks. Chopsticks were invented in China. Later, as each country of South and Southeast Asia was influenced by China, chopsticks became the primary utensils for dining there as well. Simple-looking chopsticks actually have many functions – a pair of chopsticks can meet the major dining needs. Most Chinese children begin to learn how to use chopsticks at the age of three or four.

When using chopsticks to eat, one must be aware of many things: for example, it is incorrect to place chopsticks on the table with uneven length. This is called "three long and two short", which in Chinese indicates death or misfortune and is unlucky. One may not tap chopsticks on bowls or plates, as many people think this will cause one to become as poor as a beggar. Inserting chopsticks into a rice bowl is also completely not permitted, as it looks like the incense offered at sacrifices and is therefore unlucky. In addition, using chopsticks to point at someone/something or putting them into the mouth is a taboo, and is considered a breach of "etiquette".

9.3 Banquet and Wine Ceremony

We have always been talking about eating, but actually when Chinese people treat others to a meal, it does not only involve food. Especially at formal dinners, alcohol cannot be done without. This is why Chinese people say "it's not a feast if there aren't any drinks" and often refer to the dining table at banquets as the "drinking table".

Since ancient times, China has been primarily an agricultural society, so the vast majority of alcohol is made from grain. The main types of Chinese liquor are *huangjiu* (yellow liquor) and *baijiu* (white liquor). *Huangjiu* is brewed wine unique to China. *Baijiu* is a kind of colorless distilled liquor, and is considered one of the world's four great distilled liquors along with French brandy, Russian vodka, and Scotch whiskey .

Among the three-thousand-year-old Shang Dynasty bronze ware unearthed at Anyang in Henan Province, besides tools for eating, there were also a large number of drinking vessels. This shows that alcohol played an important role in Chinese etiquette culture. During ancient sacrifices, people offered alcohol to the heaven, the earth and their ancestors, a custom which has continued to this day. Men of letters would use alcohol for inspiration when creating their works – the famous Tang Dynasty poet Li Bai was said to "drink a gallon of wine and write a hundred poems", meaning only with the alcohol, could he have been able to write good poetry.

The most important function of alcohol, of course, is at the table. After a guest is seated, the host offers him a toast, usually finishing the glass. This is a type of etiquette which embodies sincerity. After the first round, the host and guest alike can pour each other more liquor, but must fill the glass to the brim – this is yet another kind of etiquette. Drinking together in this way allows the host and guest to have deeper conversations and feelings: quite a few problems are solved in this kind of pleasant atmosphere. Naturally, those who do not drink should mention this beforehand to avoid others' displeasure.

9.4 Tea and Tea Ceremony

Tea, like silk and china, is often considered as a symbol of Chinese culture.

Drinking tea in China, just like drinking alcohol, has a very long history. During Tang Dynasty 1,000 years ago, Lu Yu wrote *The Classic of Tea*, in which he dates back the origin of tea drinking to 4,000 years ago. There are many varieties of tea, several thousand in all, and the most common ones at present are green tea, black tea, and oolong tea. Green tea is not fermented, and is best fresh. Many people who travel to Hangzhou buy Longjing tea, a famous kind of green tea. Black tea, on the other hand, is completely fermented. Black tea from Qimen in China is quite well-known. Oolong tea is half-fermented and is a distinctive Chinese form of tea; the most famous type is Tieguanyin from Anxi County. Scented teas, such as jasmine tea, are also common in Chinese daily life. They are in fact made by adding fragrant flowers into green tea or black tea, which gives them their scent.

In ancient China, drinking tea, just like eating food and drinking alcohol, was an exercise in etiquette and was later called tea ceremony. This influenced the culture of other East Asian countries as well – Japan and South Korea each have their own tea ceremony. In modern times, much of the complicated ancient ceremony has been simplified, but using tea as a medium for social behavior is still the norm. Today, the host will generally offer his/her guest a cup of tea, and most restaurants will first serve tea to customers. In the past, when formally becoming someone's pupil or apprentice, a person would offer his/her master tea; if the master accepted the tea and took a sip, that meant that he had accepted the person as his/her pupil. There was also a way to use tea to make friends, called a "tea reception", in which friends would gather together to appreciate good tea and exchange thoughts. In the present day, this has turned into the form of casual recreation known as the tea party: everyone sits together drinking tea and talking. Also, when visiting friends and relatives, tea leaves are still a common gift. Because tea leaves are so common in Chinese life, it has been said that the seven things Chinese people cannot live without are: firewood, rice, oil, salt, soy sauce, vinegar, and tea.

Lesson 10

The Various Kinships and Etiquette of Marriages, Funerals, and Rituals

10.1 Marriages and the Etiquette of Weddings

In traditional Chinese custom, wedding is an extremely important occasion for the family. When someone got married, the entire family would put all their energy into the wedding. Most families today are the same, but the ceremony have become simplified.

Although the wedding ceremony has been simplified, Chinese people still maintain many of their basic thoughts about it. In ancient China, people cared much about equal social status between the families. A matchmaker would first introduce each family's circumstances to the other, after which the parents of both would confirm the particulars of the wedding. As a result, most ancient Chinese had arranged marriages, the man and woman in question didn't have the right to decide. Now love marriage is the norm, but the idea of equal rank between families still exists. People often choose to marry someone whose family's position, economic power, and background are similar.

Traditionally, a date would be chosen on which the wedding would take place – the so-called "ecliptic auspicious day". This concept still exists among people, but it is not taken so seriously as it was in the past and has become mainly a type of psychological reassurance. For example, people often choose a date with the number eight or six. In Chinese, "eight" has a similar pronunciation to "making a fortune", and six signifies success.

On the wedding day, the man is called the bridegroom and the woman the bride. The bridegroom goes to the bride's house to accept her as his wife. In ancient times, a bridal sedan chair would be used for this, but now a long procession of festooned vehicles is used instead. In a traditional wedding, after the bridegroom brought his wife home, the couple would pay their respects with "*baitang*", which made them husband and wife. Now, though this formality is no longer observed, couples getting married still bow to their parents to show gratitude for their upbringing.

China's minority ethnic group each have some unique customs regarding marriage.

For example, kidnapping the bride in Achang ethnic group, teasing the bridegroom in Qiang ethnic group, and throwing an embroidered ball in Zhuang ethnic group, and so on. As China is a multi-ethnic country, after thousands of years of integration, many marriage customs have learned from each other. Different marriage ceremonies of each ethnic group are all a part of Chinese culture.

10.2 The Etiquette of Funerals and Sacrifice

Chinese people avoid saying the word "death" and words with similar pronunciation, such as the number four. In order to avoid saying that someone has "died", Chinese people often say that he has "passed away", "left our world", etc. This is because it is believed when someone dies, he leaves the world of the living (the *yang* world) and goes to the netherworld (the *yin* world). People refer to *yangshou* as the age in this world, and *yinshou* as the age after death. Because of the idea that dead people leave this world and go to another place to live, in ancient times, no matter the rich or the poor would all bury some of the dead person's things along with him. A large number of funerary objects discovered in the archeological studies of ancient tombs have left us many traces of the life of ancient people.

Funeral in China is particularly solemn and respectful. There are many traditional methods of burial, such as burial in the earth, cremation, celestial burial, and water burial, but the most common one is burial in the earth, often called being "laid to rest".

In fact, in ancient times, Chinese people would start to think about their funerals while still alive. People were particular about the site of the tomb, even thinking that a good or bad burial site would bring good or bad luck to their descendants. Secondly, the family would choose the coffin for an old man in advance. Even if the family is poor, people would ensure the old man a coffin. After a relative died, the family would dress the deceased in graveclothes, make the most important part of the house into a mourning hall, and be with the deceased three days and three nights in observance, which is called keeping vigil beside the coffin. After three days, the family would move the coffin to the cemetery,which is called "funeral procession". During the procession, the family would burn a lot of paper money, paper houses, paper cows, sheep, and so on. This was in the hope that the dead could live happily in the next world.

Qingming Festival (Tomb-Sweeping Day) is a Chinese holiday that occurs each year around the fifth of April. On this day, Chinese people pay their respects to the dead and visit their graves. They put some fresh dirt on the grave, pull up any weeds, set a table of food and drink, light a stick of incense, and then kowtow, pay tribute to the dead, and offer sacrifices. Some families also worship their ancestors in their houses. The custom of sweeping tombs already has a history of more than 2,500 years. Nowadays, in order to save land resources, many parts of China do not allow burial in the earth, and tomb-sweeping has gradually become a ceremony for remembering the departed.

10.3 Kinship Terminology and Relationships

It is a top priority to understand some basic norms and tattoos if you want to live with Chinese. There are still many cultural details to be understood in daily life, among which the most needed to be familiar with is how to call people according to their titles.

Paternal aunts and uncles, maternal aunts and uncles, paternal nephew, maternal nephew... Even in China, due to the simplied family structure nowadays, the younger generation also often confuses appellation. Chinese titles have been influenced by traditional thought and moral concepts: they are an important part of etiquette and also a sign of one's blood relationship, status and position. If you understand the culture of Chinese titles, it will be easier to communicate with Chinese people.

Kinship in China has a close relationship with marriage and bloodline, which can be divided into three types: those for clan relatives, maternal relatives, and one's wife's relatives. Forms of address for each type are different.

Clan relatives: the male-branch linked by the bloodline of the father

Maternal relatives: the kinsmen linked by the bloodline of the mother

Wife's relatives: the relatives linked by the wife

When addressing one's elders, one's father's father is called *yeye*, mother is called *nainai*, sisters are called *gugu*, elder brothers are called *bofu*, and younger brothers are called *shushu*; one's mother's father is called *laoye* or *waigong*, mother is called *laolao* or *waipo*, sisters are called *yi*, and brothers are called *jiujiu*. When addressing people of the same generation, one's father's relatives' children are called *tang* – a female cousin older than oneself is called *tangjie*, a male cousin younger than oneself is *tangdi*, and so on; while one's mother's relatives' children are called *biao* – a male cousin older than oneself is called *biaoge*, a female cousin younger than oneself is *biaomei*, and so on. When addressing those of a younger generation, one's brothers' descendants are called *zhizi* or *zhinü*; one's sisters' descendants are called *waisheng* or *waishengnü*.

Also, correctly addressing one's parents-in-law is also very important, as there are different forms of address. Husbands refer to their wives' parents as *yuefu* (or *zhangren*) and *yuemu* (or *zhangmuniang*); wives refer to their husbands' parents as *gongong* and *popo*. However, when one's parent-in-law is present, one calls him/her father and mother as one's husband or wife does. A husband's parents refer to their daughter-in-law as *erxifu*, and wife's parents refer to their son-in-law as *nüxu* or *guye*.

There is a great difference in the forms of address between husband and wife of the ancient times and of today. In ancient times, a husband would call his wife *furen* or *niangzi*, and a wife would call her husband *fujun* or *xianggong*, but to other people, the wife would be called *jiannei* or *zhuojing*, both of which denoted modesty. Nowadays, such titles have been simplified, and husband and wife can address each other by name, or by the relatively affectionate *laogong* and *laopo*.

When siblings get married, there are special ways to describe the relationship between their spouses. For example, *zhouli* refers to wives of brothers, and *lianjin* refers to husbands of sisters.

Perhaps, after reading this, you are a bit confused. But these are only the most basic kinship terms for Chinese. If we add in other relatives, it gets even more complicated. From this, we can feel that Chinese people pay close attention to the idea of "family". Each member of the family obtains a fixed position at home and a specialized title. Attaching great importance to family and blood relations is a particularly important part of traditional Chinese culture.

10.4 Honorific and Modest Titles

In addition to the title in the family, a person also has some special titles too due to his different roles or statuses in the society.

In ancient society, an emperor's status was the highest, while officials were ranked by their positions. Commoners could never address the emperor or any official by his name. Likewise, those of low status or young age could not call their elders or superiors by name.

To the emperor, one could say *bixia*, *shengshang*, or *huangshang*, and the emperor would call himself *zhen*, *gu*, or *guaren*. When speaking to the emperor, officials referred to themselves as *chen* or *weichen*. Minor officials would call more important officials *daren* and refer to themselves as *xiaguan* or *xiaoren*, while commoners called all officials *daren* and themselves *xiaoren*. This kind of complex system of titles may seem unthinkable to people of today, but it was imperative to ancients to use correct titles lest they fail to observe the proprieties.

Today, to address a man respectfully, you can call him *xiansheng* and a woman *nüshi*, but these forms of address did not exist in traditional Chinese title. At that time, *xiansheng* and *shifu* referred only to teachers. Now, calling someone Mr. Wang or Master Zhang is a way of expressing politeness or respect, even though the other party might not actually be a master.

Some Westerners may directly address their parents or elders by name, but this is absolutely not absolutely permissible in Chinese culture. In traditional society, one would call one's father and mother *fuqin* and *muqin*, or *fuqin daren* and *muqin daren*, respectively, and to others would refer to them as *jiafu* and *jiamu*, while calling others' parents *lingzun* and *lingtang*. Nowadays, though some older people still prefer to use these terms, young Chinese simply call parents mom and dad.

Modest titles are the opposite of honorific titles. They are used to refer to oneself as a way of expressing modesty. For example, ancient Chinese men called themselves *bucai*, *zaixia*, or *wansheng* and women *qieshen* or *nujia*, and so on, while children were referred to as *quanzi* and *xiaonü*. The titles *xiaoren*, *xiaguan*, and *weichen* mentioned in the previous section can also be considered modest titles. Today, such expressions are rarely used, but on extremely formal occasions, one can occasionally hear such a modest title as *zaixia*.

10.5 The Family Taboo and National Taboo

There is another interesting phenomenon in China called taboo. When addressing people of high rank or advanced age, Chinese people avoid using their names to show their respect, for which reason it is called the naming taboo. The most important taboos are the national taboo and family taboo. The national taboo was that one must avoid using the name of any of the emperors of the present dynasty, and the family taboo was that one must avoid using the name of one's elders in the family.

The national taboo was adhered to even by the emperor himself. For example, the father of Qinshihuang, the first emperor of China, was named Chu, which happened also to be the name of a part of China. After Qin unified China, he changed the name of that area to Jing. Even today, a part of Hubei Province in the middle reaches of the Yangtze River is still called the land of Jingchu. The name of Li Shimin, Emperor Taizong in Tang Dynasty, included the character "min", which was also the name of a part of the government, *Minbu* (Ministry of Households). That ministry was thus renamed *Hubu* (Ministry of Revenue). If one did not respect the national taboo, it was considered a great crime, for which one could be imprisoned or even killed.

The family taboo, also called the private taboo, was actually an extension of the national taboo. As mentioned above, if a Chinese person calls his father or elders by name, it was considered a major breach of etiquette. The father of the Tang Dynasty poet Du Fu was named Xian, so while Du Fu wrote more than 1,400 poems in his lifetime, not one of them contains the character "xian".

Today, although strict naming taboos have disappeared, the idea behind them still exerts a subtle influence over the rules regarding forms of address and titles.

Lesson 11

Regulations on Talent Selection

11.1 Recommending People Noted for Filial Piety and Morality and the Nine-Rank System of Meritocracy of Selecting Officials

It requires talents first to govern a country. Since ancient times, all the state administrators laid emphasis on the selection of talents. There are related records about it in *The Rites of Zhou*, "there was a general competition every three years", namely to select talents every three years to supplement the management departments. 2,000 years ago, Han Dynasty was centralized, unified and stable. State administrators implemented a kind of system of personnel selection and employment called "personnel evaluation and recommendation", recommending people with noble morality and outstanding ability for posts of state governance. The items of the personnel examination were various, among which the most important ones were filial piety and morality, which meant to respect and be obedient to the parents, and be fair and upright in actions. Only those with these qualities could be selected as officials. Regarding filial piety as the most important quality reflects the status of the family in ancient Chinese state governance.

Though it did meet the requirements of "the rule of ritual" to select those who are filial and of high morality as officials, but in practice, the ones rated as the filial and moral were the sons of noble or rich families, and it was difficult for ordinary people to enter into the state governance. In the Three Kingdoms Period (220-280), Cao Pi, Emperor Wen of Wei Kingdom introduced the nine-rank system of meritocracy which advocated employing people based on their good merits, aiming to get access to talents as soon as possible. However, aristocratic families soon used this approach to get higher positions in the government.

11.2 The Imperial Examination Lasting for a Thousand of Years and Its Influence

How to truly get talents in a huge country? This problem became more and more formidable as time went by. About this case, 1,400 years ago, the administrators in the Sui and Tang dynasties came up with the imperial examination system, an examination project completely different from the previous selecting mechanism. In the long history of later dynasties, this system had continually been transformed, adjusted and improved, and not abolished until 1905.

The imperial examination broke down the dominance of powerful and rich families over official positions, making a ladder for ordinary people to climb. As a Tang poem goes: "A farmer working in the fields in the early morning, became an official in the imperial palace in the evening". There had finally appeared a channel between the upper gentry and the common people. Though not broad, it had always been unblocked, and continually transmitting fresh blood to the reservoir of national talents, thus refreshing a bit the growing rigid administration mechanism.

The system had been implemented for more than 1,000 years, and accumulated extremely rich experience and wisdom for talent selection and examination systems, and its shadow can still be seen in many practices done in the college entrance examinations and the civil service examination in modern China. This system has not only deeply affected Japan, South Korea, Vietnam and other East and Southeast Asian countries, but also the civil service systems established in Western countries.

The talents were developed and selected through a set of sophisticated selection system, to be assigned into posts of the organizations of the government. Hence, since ancient times, Chinese scholars have believed in the notion that "He who excels in learning would end up being an official", and the ideal of "cultivating both the body and spirit, conducting both the family and the state, placating the world under the sky", aspiring to be recognized in the state's bureaucratic system and be promoted step by step.

11.3 From the Three Councillors and Nine Ministers of the State to the Three Departments and Six Ministries

Qinshihuang united China in 221 BC. From 221 BC to 1911 AD, the centralized imperial system had been in practice in China for about 2,000 years, in the accompany of a set of sophisticated bureaucratic system.

In the central government, there implemented the system of three councillors and nine ministers in the Qin and Han dynasties. The term "three councillors" existed since ancient times, referring to the three highest official ranks in the management system, but each corresponding to different posts in different dynasties, and the nine ministers referred to important official ranks in the central government, but with no conformity in different dynasties. So, "three councillors and nine ministers" had been more of the systematic summary of the experience in governance undergone by previous nations before Qin Dynasty.

The central bureaucracy had formed a well-organized system, named the Three Departments and Six Ministries. The Three Departments were *Zhongshu* Department, *Menxia* Department and *Shangshu* Department, and the Six Ministries were Ministry of Official Personnel Affairs, Ministry of Revenue, Ministry of Rites, Ministry of War, Ministry of Punishments, and Ministry of Public Works. The Three Departments and Six Ministries system had constantly been adjusted and transformed in the subsequent vicissitudes of dynasties, and gradually become more and more completed, detailed and sophisticated, but not completely abolished until the end of Qing Dynasty, and its operation mechanism had reached a very high level.

11.4 From the System of Prefectures and Counties to the System of Provincial Governance

Most places in China had been implementing the system of prefectures and counties before Qinshihuang united China. After Qin Dynasty unified the whole country and adopted the two-level system of prefectures and counties, local officials were appointed and removed by the central government, and local administrations were always under the jurisdiction of the central government. At the end of Eastern Han Dynasty, it was shaped into the three-level system of states, prefectures and counties. Since then, both the two-level and the three-level systems of the local administrative management patterns had been similar to each other, especially the county-level administrations, which have been implementing for more than 2,000 years, and are still the basic administrative units of the country now.

The provincial administrations have begun in Yuan Dynasty (1271-1368), which meant, the central government was in charge of state affairs by Zhongshu Ministry, and its agent, the executive secretariat (provincial administration) in charge of local administration. The establishment of the provincial administration system has formed the rudiment of modern local administrative divisions in China. Although Ming Dynasty renamed major provinces as chief envoys, they were still customarily called “provinces”. Since then, “province” has always been the highest local administrative division in China, and has been adopted until now.

Lesson 12

It's Impolite Not to Reciprocate

12.1 Silk Road and Trade

The Silk Road is a famous land trade route which came into being more than 2,000 years ago during the Western Han Period. It ran from Chang'an (now Xi'an in Shaanxi Province), China's capital at the time, all the way to Roman Empire. Han Dynasty's silk, tea, and the technology for smelting, irrigation, and silk all spread to the West on this road, while Western fur, jewels, and spices came to China. Of the many Chinese products transported to the West at that time, those made from silk had the greatest effect, from which fact the road got its name.

From then until Ming Dynasty some 1,500 years later, though it was intermittent, the Silk Road had always been an important passage between China and other countries in Europe and Asia. Over the long history, many famous people have had some relationship with the road. The Western Han official Zhang Qian was the pioneer of the Silk Road; the Tang Dynasty monk Xuanzang traveled to India to study and brought back many scriptures, influencing Buddhism of all East Asia; and the Italian merchant Marco Polo toured China for seventeen years and told Europe about it, stirring up European dreams of the East. We can imagine a scene on the Silk Road: scholars and merchants on horsebacks, leading caravans of camels, riding through the desert and gobi, stopping to rest their legs when they see water and trees. Places with water were oases, some of which slowly became beautiful villages. The famous Dunhuang was originally a beautiful village like this, which left exquisite frescoes for later generations.

Corresponding to the land Silk Road is the maritime Silk Road. It developed over 2,000 years ago in the Qin and Han periods, but flourished 1,000 years ago during the Song Dynasty. Porcelain was then gradually becoming the main item of trade, so the maritime Silk Road was called by some the "Ceramic Road".

With the help of trade, Chinese silk and porcelain were constantly transported to other countries. Many years later, these elegant objects became a part of local people's life.

Meanwhile, products from other countries also continuously entered China and have enriched the lives of Chinese people. Tomatoes, watermelons, sweet potatoes, carrots, peppers are common on Chinese dining tables. One can tell their origin from their names since *xi*, *fan* and *hu* all mean "foreign".

12.2 Long Voyages and International Relations

In the Warring States Period more than 2,000 years ago, the vast expanse of China contained many vassal states, which all communicated with one another very frequently. However, transportation was not very developed at that time, and took place mostly between neighboring countries. After Qinshihuang united China, the scope of diplomacy expanded accordingly. During Eastern Han Dynasty, the king of Wonu in Japan sent envoys to China, and accepted the "Han King of Wonu" golden official seal from Emperor Guangwu of Han Dynasty. On the western front, there are also records of diplomatic envoys sent between Eastern Han and Daqin.

Tang Dynasty enjoyed a booming economy and advanced culture, and communication between China and countries in the West and East was frequent. Japan dispatched envoys to Tang Dynasty thirteen times to study Chinese culture and institutions, and envoys from Dashi of the Middle East were sent to China more than thirty times.

During Ming Dynasty, Zheng He was sent to sea seven times by the emperor, each time leading enormous fleets of ships. He reached countries in Southeast Asia, South Asia, and Africa. When he returned, he also invited many kings and officials from other countries to China. The ability shown by Zheng He's voyages to the West Seas was unparalleled in the world at that time.

The contributions of Zheng He's sailing the seas were left in *Zheng He's Nautical Chart*, but explorations of the seas were declined after the ban on maritime activities in Ming Dynasty. In Qing Dynasty, China began to adopt a stricter policy of sealing itself off from foreign contact, and its relations with other countries became sparse.

12.3 Mutual Cultural Communication

Cultural exchange between ancient China and other countries not only refers to the introduction of foreign cultures represented by Buddhism, but also the influence of China on its neighboring countries.

Buddhism began in ancient India, and was introduced to the central plains of China at the end of Western Han Dynasty, and during the Southern and Northern Dynasties, it was promoted and reached its peak. Many of the statues and grottoes we see today were made at that time. In Tang Dynasty, Buddhism continued to thrive, and two great monks made an enormous contributions to its dissemination.

The first was Xuanzang, who underwent countless hardships to travel to Tianzhu (the present-day India), the holy land of Buddhism. There he met eminent monks, studied Buddhism, translated scriptures, and brought back many Buddhist classics, thus having a great effect on its development in China. His experience was recorded in *The Great Tang Records of the Western Regions*, which was a priceless document. One of Chinese Four Class Works, *Journey to the West*, is also based on his experience.

Jianzhen was another famous monk from Tang Dynasty. He made six eastward trips to Japan before successfully arriving at it, and lived there for ten years spreading Buddhism and Chinese culture. Even today, Japanese make offerings to his statue.

Now Buddhism has been an inseparable part of Chinese culture. Many vocabulary and idioms are taken from it. For example, the Chinese words for "world, masses, truth, inconceivable, enlightenment, forewarning", and more are all Buddhist in origin. There are also many sayings or proverbs with Buddhist influences.

Cultural exchanges are always two-way. While actively accepting and integrating foreign cultures, China has also been constantly influencing neighboring countries, such as Chinese characters. Even today, we can still see Chinese characters in Japanese language, and Vietnam, South Korea, and North Korea used Chinese characters until just a century ago. This is what is known as the Sinosphere. In Japanese, Korean, and Vietnamese, one can hear many words whose pronunciation is quite similar to that of Chinese, because they were borrowed from Chinese. Beyond this, their festivals, traditional medicine, architectural style, and many other aspects have also been deeply influenced by China.

Unit 4 Harmony

Lesson 13

Harmony Brings Prosperity

13.1 Customs of Celebrating the New Year

Spring Festival is the first day of the new year on the Chinese calendar, and the day before the festival is called the New Year's Eve, during which the whole family will come together to enjoy a reunion dinner to ring out the old year and ring in the new year. At this time, many places in China, especially in northern China, dumplings are indispensable to the dining table, while New Year cakes are favored by southern Chinese. Beginning in the 1980s, in addition to the New Year's Eve dinner, there is also a TV program called the Spring Festival Gala to celebrate the Spring Festival. This New Year's party features singing and dancing, crosstalk, opusculum, magic, acrobatics, opera, and other art forms to create an atmosphere for joyous reunion.

During the Spring Festival, every family puts up Spring Festival couplets and New Year pictures. Spring Festival couplets are two matched lines of auspicious words written with a writing brush on red paper and placed on the left and right sides of the front door. After seeing them outside, you can come in and see the New Year pictures. These pictures are unlike Chinese paintings – the topics are obvious and the colors gorgeous and exaggerated. Like this picture, *The Mouse Gets Married*: a group of mice are noisily carrying the bride's sedan chair to the bridegroom's house, but he unexpectedly turns out to be a cat. That he should eat all the mice is the simple aspiration of the hard-working laborers.

During the Spring Festival, the most common custom is going to the temple fair. The temple fair originated from religious sacrifical activities, but later it gradually became a recreational gathering. The styles of temple fairs vary from place to place, but they all have a great variety of performances, delicious snacks, and colorful artcraft. Therefore, it has become the most lively custom during the Spring Festival.

13.2 Yuanxiao and Lanterns

It is called "*guonian*" (the celebration of the new year) from the first day to the fifteenth day of the first lunar month in China, and the fifteenth day of the first lunar month is the Lantern Festival, which is not only the last day of "*guonian*", but also the first full moon day of the whole year. On this day, people eat *yuanxiao*, also called *tangyuan* in south China, which is a dish of round balls within whose skin contain all kinds of delicious fillings. Both the names *yuanxiao* and *tangyuan* are imbued with the meaning of "reunion".

The main celebrating activity of Lantern Festival is enjoying lanterns. During the festival, all kinds of colored lanterns beautifully decorate the night. At this time, if you see someone under the lanterns looking up, they are probably guessing lantern riddles. Lantern riddles are riddles written on the top of lanterns; you can enjoy the colorful lights and guess the riddles simultaneously. Actually, it was with special and beautiful expectations that the ancients set up lantern riddles during the festival. Ouyang Xiu, a famous tune writer of Song Dynasty, had written in one of his tunes that: "Last year on lunar festive night, lanterns mid blooms shone as daylight. When the moon rose atop willow trees, my lover had a tryst with me." Apparently, in ancient times, Lantern Festival was like a traditional Valentine's Day, a day when pre-destined persons meet each other.

13.3 Mid-Autumn Festival and Reunion

The fifteenth day of the eight month on the lunar calendar is the Mid-Autumn Festival. As the name suggests, this day is in the middle of autumn, during which the weather is cool and comfortable. On this night, the moon is bright and round, which symbolizes reunion. It is a time when children far away from home come back to reunite with parents. Meanwhile, the ancients thought the movement of the moon was closely related to the harvest of crops, so they formed the custom of worshipping the moon and offering oblations to the moon on this day. The folk legends of Chang'e flying to the moon and Jade Rabbit pounding herbs have been handed down to this day. Innumerable poets had written quantities of poems expressing missing emotions through the moon, such as "Looking up, I find the moon bright; Bowing, in homesickness I'm drowned" (*Thoughts on a Tranquil Night* by Li Bai), "Over the sea grows the moon bright; we gaze on it far, far apart" (*Looking at the Moon and Longing for One Far away* by Zhang Jiuling).

Moon cake has always been the main food for Mid-Autumn Festival. The stuffed dough is pressed into a flat pastry, and baked to be golden moon cakes. While eating the moon cakes, it is really like holding a full moon in your palm. The round moon cake of course conveys the meaning of "reunion".

Lesson 14

Harmony in Diversity

14.1 Confucianism and Confucius and Mencius

Confucianism is not a religion; it is more of a school of thought with Confucius as its founder. Confucius lived in the Spring and Autumn Period around the year 500 BC, at which time China was composed of many vassal states whose rulers all hoped to find someone to help them administer their land. Confucius first traveled around several states, hoping to gain entrance into the officialdom and thereby implement his political ideas. Afterward he found that his political thought would be extremely hard to put into practice, so he returned to his hometown and opened his doors to pupils, hoping in that way to spread his political thought. It is said that Confucius had 3,000 pupils, of whom seventy-two were outstanding. Later generations put the words and ideas of Confucius and his disciples in a book called *The Analects of Confucius*, and the book has a great influence on Chinese thought.

At the core of Confucian thought are "benevolence (*ren*) " and "proprieties (*li*)". The basis of "benevolence" is love for mankind; it stresses that we must learn to put ourselves in others' position and to treat others as we would be treated. "Do not impose on others what you yourself do not desire". And "proprieties", or etiquette, aim to mediate interpersonal relationships and make them more harmonious, i.e. "The use of proprieties is to make interpersonal relationship more harmonious".

Another important figure in the formation of Confucianism is Mencius. He was born a century after Confucius, but his life story was quite similar with that of Confucius. Mencius was quite eloquent and moved about the states trying to persuade rulers to use a strict moral code to constrain themselves while hoping they would love common people and develop production. However, his ideas were also not thought highly of by those rulers. They were later recorded in the book *Mencius* and circulated.

In fact, both Confucius and Mencius lived in an important age of enlightenment in Chinese history: society underwent great transformations and different schools of thought coexisted with intense debate and competition among them. The doctrine of Confucianism was just one of many schools of thought at the time, but after 100 years, it found favor with the highest ruler of Han Dynasty, and gradually became the orthodox school of thought in China. Successive dynasties continually solidified the tradition and even turned the classic writings of Confucianism into prescribed texts for imperial examinations. Hence Confucianism has had a deep and lasting impact on Chinese values, ways of thinking, and national character. For more than 2,000 years, as Confucianism advocates, Chinese people have held a sense of propriety, respected established norms, and pursued the golden mean.

14.2 Taoism and Laozi

The Big Bang hypothesis supposes that the universe started as something extremely dense and hot, and after continuous expansion, gradually evolved into its present form. Laozi, the founder of Taoism, proposed a similar explanation over 2,000 years ago. According to him, the universe at first was empty, and myriad things were gradually formed in the order of one becoming two, two becoming three, and so on.

After reading this so far, you might already have discovered that compared to Confucius, Laozi seems more like a philosopher. What he thought about was the law of movement of the heaven and the earth, the universe and everything. He called this law "tao" and said that it has no form, that it is invisible and untouchable, yet it exists everywhere and contains within it all things. This understanding of the essence of things is the basis of Taoist theory. Referring to this law, he said that people are included in "myriad things", and so should follow the natural order instead of interfering with it. This attitude is as natural as a ditch forming where water flows.

"Tao" which Laozi talked about is invisible and indescribable, so Taoism has always had a sort of mysterious character. For this reason, a religion gradually formed in Eastern Han Dynasty. This is Taoism, a religion which formed natively in China with a set of pedigreed immortal beings. Throughout history, Taoism has had a great attraction among common people: it tells them that through long-time cultivation, they can become immortal beings. This is commonly referred to as "*dedao chengxian*" among Chinese folks.

Taoism has had a large influence on Chinese aesthetics. Chinese people's endeavor to find in art for the connection between the form and the spirit, between the real and the fake, and so on all comes from Taoism. Among the people, the development of Taoism also gave rise to a Taoist holy land in China – Mount Wudang, which was associated with Wudang kung fu, one of the most important schools of Chinese martial arts.

14.3 The Assimilation of Buddhism

Buddhism originated from ancient India in the 6th century BC and was introduced to China around Han Dynasty. With the prosperity of the Silk Road, the Mogao Caves in Dunhuang along the Hexi Corridor gradually became a treasure house of Buddhist art. Here you can read stories from the Buddhist classics on the beautiful frescoes and appreciate Buddha statues ranging in height from thirty meters to only several centimeters. If all the works of art in the Mogao Caves were lined up, they would form an art gallery 25 kilometers long.

South of Dunhuang in Sichuan, you can find the world's largest stone Buddha statue – Leshan Giant Buddha. This statue, completely cut from a precipice, is 71 meters in height and took 90 years to complete. Eyes alone are not enough to appreciate this Buddha – you can walk along the boardwalk on the mountain to the base of the statue and stand on his foot that can hold more than 100 people. If you raise your head and look up, you will see that Buddha is the mountain and the mountain is Buddha.

There are many Buddhist constructions like Mogao Caves and Leshan Giant Buddha in China, not to mention the ubiquitous temples. Many Chinese who believe in Buddhism go to temples to light incense and pray, but those who take the tonsure and become monks and nuns are few. Chinese people are influenced more by Confucianism and are thus more pragmatic, caring about life itself. After many conflicts, the foreign religion of Buddhism has gradually merged together with Confucianism and Taoism, and influence the spiritual world of Chinese people. In past dynasties, when scholars seeking honor and official rank came across setbacks in reality, they would often pay a visit to old temples deep in the mountains and talk with the monks in search of relief. Some even returned to the fields and lived peacefully and simply like Taoist hermits.

Lesson 15

All Things Are Opposite and Unified

15.1 Yin and Yang and the Five Elements

Besides the black and white of the *yin-yang* symbol, you can find *yin* and *yang* in other things as well. For example, the heaven and the earth, the sun and the moon, men and women, moving and resting. Chinese people thought of the concepts of *yin* and *yang* from these phenomena and used these concepts to understand the world. For example, a cloudy day when the sun is not visible is called a "*yin* day"; protruding characters cut into a seal are called "*yang* characters"; an open ditch for draining water is called a "*yang* drain" while a closed one is called a "*yin* drain", and so on. Also, *yin* and *yang* are opposite to each other, but when they reach their height, they change places. For example, hot is *yang* and cold is *yin*. However, after the hot summer, it gets cold, and after the cold winter, it gets warm. It can be said that *yin* and *yang* are all-pervasive forces in life; they are the most direct embodiment of Chinese dialectical thought.

The Five Elements are another way for Chinese people to observe the world. Ancient people summed up all basic materials into five types: metal, wood, water, fire and soil. The elements can generate one another and also overcome one another. For example, water can generate wood, as water has a positive effect on wood; and fire can overcome wood, as fire has a destructive effect on it. Like *yin* and *yang*, Chinese people relate the Five Elements to other phenomena in life such as orientations, positions, numbers, colors, and seasons. Take orientations for example. The Five Elements theory claims that water is in the north, fire is in the south, wood is in the east, metal is in the west, and soil is in the center.

15.2 Traditional Chinese Medicine

Traditional Chinese medicine was formed on the basis of *yin* and *yang* and the Five Elements. It claims that there are two forces (*qi*, sometimes written *chi* or *ki*), one *yin* and one *yang* moving in the body, and the five sense organs and five internal organs (heart, liver, spleen, lungs, and kidneys) correspond to the Five Elements. Thus an imbalance of *yin* and *yang* within the body will cause pathological changes in the internal organs and reflect in the external organs. For example, traditional Chinese medicine claims kidneys are water, containing one's vitality and energy, and are interlinked with the ears, so hearing loss and tinnitus are symptoms of unhealthy kidneys. Traditional Chinese medicine treats not only the symptoms, but also the disease.

The medicines used are comprised mainly of plants, animals, and minerals, with plants the most important. As a result, they are also known as "herbal medicines". Li Shizhen, the Ming Dynasty medical scholar, spent over 30 years to complete the masterwork *Compendium of Materia Medica*, which includes 1,892 kinds of medicine and 11,096 prescriptions and can be considered a summary of the thousands of years of traditional Chinese medicine. Ginseng, pilous antlers, and cordyceps are precious medicinal materials, but most materials can be found in daily life, such as lotus seeds, chrysanthemums, soybeans, and honey.

Aside from medicine, Chinese began to use another method of treatment: acupuncture 5,000 years ago. Traditional Chinese medicine discovered in the body twelve main and eight supplementary channels. These channels are like an invisible road stringing together the acupuncture points, the places where *qi* moves and rests. By using hands, needles, or heat at these points, *qi* can be made to move normally again, thus restoring the balance of *yin* and *yang* in the body.

15.3 Taijiquan and Chinese Kung Fu

Besides Chinese medicine, the theory of *yin* and *yang* also has a close relationship with

China's unique form of exercise – *taijiquan*. *Taijiquan* is very popular among Chinese people. It is not only the first choice for martial arts enthusiasts, but also a common form for ordinary people alike to stay healthy.

The currently popular *taijiquan* is generally believed to have originated 400 years ago from Chen-style *taijiquan* in Chenjiagou, Henan Province, after which different schools were formed. But no matter which school it belongs to, the goal of *taijiquan* is the same: to adjust the breathing and limbs through a peaceful rhythm, and in the end to balance *yin* and *yang*. Stretching exercises complement slow, gradual breathing, which makes it easy to appreciate *taijiquan*. In certain important events, one can see performances of thousands and even ten thousands of people practicing *taijiquan* together.

Taijiquan can be considered a representative of Chinese kung fu, but there are actually many other kinds as well. The kung fu star Bruce Lee practiced *taijiquan*, wing chun, and mantis boxing since childhood. Also, we should separate kung fu from martial arts: kung fu does not simply mean external actions, but includes training the body with *qigong*, a system of breathing exercises. The saying goes "on the outside you practice your muscles and skin, and on the inside you practice your spirit and *qi*". When we admire Shaolin kung fu, we cannot ignore that they went through ten years of strenuous study and exercise. As a result, kung fu actually merges *zhonghe* in confucianism with *shoujing* in Taoism and *zen* in Buddhism. In a sense, Chinese kung fu is the external embodiment of traditional Chinese thought.

15.4 The Book of Changes and the Eight Diagrams

Let's look at another important classic related to *yin* and *yang* – *The Book of Changes*. In Shang Dynasty, oracle bone scripts found on tortoise shells and animal bones were used for divination. Major events like sacrifices, marriages, expeditions, and campaigns all required divination beforehand, and *The Book of Changes* was such a record of these oracle inscriptions.

The most important concept of the book is the Eight Diagrams, whose philosophical basis is *yin* and *yang*. This symbol (⚊) represents *yang* and (⚋) represents *yin*. Divinatory trigrams are made from three such symbols in a row. For example, the *qian* trigram (☰) is made from three *yang*s and represents the heaven, and the *kun* trigram (☷) is made from three *yins*, representing the earth.

Ancient people made a detailed interpretation of the Eight Diagrams. For example, people can be enlightened from the heaven and the earth trigrams: a person must struggle constantly, like the constant movement of the heaven; but must also be broad-minded and lenient, like the earth forming myriad things. For this reason, the book not only provides people with knowledge of the world and the universe, but also instructs people to train themselves morally and philosophically. Even the sage Confucius, after reading *The Book of Changes* in his later years, lamented that if he could only read it at the age of 50, he would not have made major mistakes.

Lesson 16

The Unity of the Heaven and Human

16.1 Fengshui and Environment

Perhaps the most direct embodiment of "the unity of the heaven and human" is the Chinese *fengshui* theory. If you watched the opening ceremony for 2008 Beijing Olympic Games, you must remember the 29 "footprint" fireworks following the central axis of the city all the way to the Bird's Nest. That central axis runs north-south and splits Beijing's West City and East City in perfect symmetry. This kind of design is a form of *fengshui*.

Since ancient times, when Chinese lay out cities or build houses, the first thing they look into is not building materials, but the building site's terrain, source of water, wind direction, soil property, orientation, and so on. These together can be known as *fengshui*. The essence of *fengshui* is searching for harmony between people and nature. At the same time, people believe that good *fengshui* is able to bring them peace and wealth. Geomancy is an ancient profession, and geomancers would look at the things all around, use a compass to be sure of the position, use a Luban ruler to measure distance, and help people pick a location with good *fengshui*. Generally, a place with auspicious geomantic omens and its surroundings is well-coordinated. The magnificently built Imperial Palace, the Summer Palace with beautiful scenery, and the exquisitely designed Hongcun Village all can be called good *fengshui*.

16.2 Temple of Heaven and Offering Sacrifices to the Heaven

The idea of the unity of the heaven and man, includes harmony with nature as well as awe and respect for the heaven. The heaven is above us, and people should follow its laws in doing work, or disasters will drop from the clouds. Ancient rulers were also bound by awe and respect for the heaven. The emperor had to announce that he was the son of the heaven before the masses would accept him. When a new emperor would ascend to the throne, he would have to begin the rite of worshiping the heaven. Temple of Heaven in Beijing was constructed for this purpose.

If you go southeast from the Imperial Palace, you will arrive at Temple of Heaven. It is as big as four Imperial Palaces, and is designed along Beijing's north-south central axis. Hall of Prayer for Good Harvests at the north end is the symbolic construction of Temple of Heaven, and you can find it in many travel brochures or guidebooks. The top of Hall of Prayer for Good Harvests is made from blue glazed tiles and merges into the sky when seen from a distance. Circular Mound Altar is at the south end, made from three concentric circles. As you approach, it gets taller and taller. If you stand on the circular slab stone right in the middle and gently shout, you will immediately hear the echoes from all sides. On Winter Solstice, the emperor would make sacrifices to the heaven here. You can imagine the solemn atmosphere of the worship ceremony, the sonorous speech and the endless echoes, as though some prophecy were being read aloud. It makes one feel the greatness of the heaven and the minuteness of man.

16.3 The Layout of Quadrangle Courtyards

If you sit in a pedicab traveling through the *hutong* of Beijing's Houhai, you will see on both sides some square courtyards – namely, quadrangle courtyards, or *siheyuan*. The quadrangle courtyards look like the Chinese character "口", with right angles and symmetry of the right and left sides. *Si* means "four", or the four directions of north, south, east, and west; *he* means to join together on the four sides, with an enclosed courtyard in the middle. If we recall the Imperial Palace mentioned above, we might notice that though it was mangnificently built, it was actually a deluxe quadrangle courtyard.

Quadrangle courtyards are the main form of Chinese traditional housing. The rooms on four sides each have meanings: elders of the family live in the principal rooms on the north side, the younger generations live on both sides of the east wing-rooms, and the rooms on the south side are next to the door and are used as the servant's room or guest room. Such a layout makes many generations of one family live together and creates harmony and joy. Apart from the living area, the courtyard has a relatively large area, where people plant flowers or raise fish in a cozy and pleasant environment, developing into an architectural form that is independent but closely related with nature.

A quadrangle courtyard conveys Chinese people's ideal of life, i.e., a happy family in harmony with nature.

16.4 Dragons and the Unity of the Heaven and Human

Chinese people claim themselves to be the descendants of dragons. But as many people know, dragon is an imaginary animal created from parts of many animals: the body of a snake, the scales of a fish, the antlers of a deer, the talons of an eagle, and the beard of a tiger. As a totem, dragon appears in many buildings and works of art.

This imaginary animal has for a long time stood for the emperor in Chinese history. People believed that dragon is the voice of the heaven, that he can fly from the deepest sea high up into the sky and create the rain needed in agriculture. In ancient agricultural society, whenever there was a great drought, people would go to the Longwang Temple and pray for rain. From respect and awe for the heaven to respect and awe for dragon – the next step is obviously respect and awe for the "Descendant of the Dragon and Son of Heaven", or the emperor. In this way, respect for nature has been turned into respect for a person. Thus dragon can also be considered a symbol of the unity of the heaven and man.

A dragon's form being an amalgamation of so many animals also reflects ancient Chinese people's wish for the merger of myriad things of nature. The idea that man and nature must find harmony you have seen in the lives of the residents of Hongcun Village, experienced in the practice of *taijiquan*, and heard at Circular Mound Altar of Temple of Heaven.

附录02

生词表

New Words and Expressions

B

生词	拼音	英文翻译	课序
把持	bǎchí	to control; to keep under control	11.1
拜师	bàishī	to formally acknowledge somebody as one's master	9.4
包办	bāobàn	to take everything on oneself	10.1
宝库	bǎokù	treasure house	14.3
宝石	bǎoshí	gemstone	12.1
爆炸	bàozhà	to explode	14.2
奔走	bēnzǒu	to be busy running about	14.1
本草	běncǎo	Chinese materia medica	15.2
本身	běnshēn	itself	14.3
陛下	bìxià	Your Majesty	10.4
避讳	bìhuì	taboo	10.2
变革	biàngé	to transform; to change	9.1
遍及	biànjí	all over	14.3
辩证	biànzhèng	dialectical	15.1

病变	bìngbiàn	to be diseased	15.2
博大	bódà	broad and profound	15.4
卜辞	bǔcí	oracle inscriptions of Shang Dynasty on tortoise shells or animal bones	15.4
布局	bùjú	layout	16.1

C

生词	拼音	英文翻译	课序
菜系	càixì	style of cooking	9.1
菜肴	càiyáo	cooked food (usually meat and fish dishes)	9.1
阐述	chǎnshù	to state	14.2
长廊	chángláng	gallery	14.3
场景	chǎngjǐng	scene	12.1
朝向	cháoxiàng	orientation	16.1
称谓	chēngwèi	form of address; appellation	10.3
诚意	chéngyì	sincerity	9.3
充实	chōngshí	substantial; rich	11.2
初	chū	at the beginning of	13.2
出殡	chūbìn	to carry a coffin to the cemetery	10.2
出嫁	chūjià	(of a woman) to get married	13.1
出众	chūzhòng	outstanding; exceptional	11.1
雏形	chúxíng	embryonic form	11.4
储藏	chǔcáng	to save and preserve	15.2

穿行	chuānxíng	to pass through	16.3
传达	chuándá	to convey; to transmit	13.1
创始人	chuàngshǐrén	founder	14.1
创意	chuàngyì	creativity	16.1
辞旧迎新	cíjiù-yíngxīn	to ring out the old year and ring in the new year	13.1
从天而降	cóngtiān'érjiàng	to drop from the sky; very unexpectedly	16.2
挫折	cuòzhé	setback	14.3

D

生词	拼音	英文翻译	课序
代言人	dàiyánrén	spokesperson	16.4
单纯	dānchún	purely; merely	9.3
当头棒喝	dāngtóu-bànghè	a blow and a shout; a sharp warning	12.3
档	dǎng	*a measure word for programs*	13.1
得道成仙	dédào-chéngxiān	to be immortal	14.2
德行	déxíng	moral integrity	15.4
登基	dēngjī	to ascend the throne	16.2
地形	dìxíng	terrain; landform	16.1
鼎盛	dǐngshèng	in a period of great prosperity	12.3
独具特色	dújù-tèsè	unique; peculiar	9.1
对立	duìlì	to oppose; to be antagonistic to	15.1
对应	duìyìng	corresponding	15.1

E

生词	拼音	英文翻译	课序
噩运	èyùn	bad luck	10.2
耳鸣	ěrmíng	tinnitus	15.2

F

生词	拼音	英文翻译	课序
发酵	fājiào	fermentation	9.4
发扬	fāyáng	to develop; to promote; to carry forward	12.3
番薯	fānshǔ	sweet potato	12.1
繁多	fánduō	a rich variety of	13.1
饭局	fànjú	dinner party	9.2
方方正正	fāngfāngzhèngzhèng	square	16.3
废除	fèichú	to abolish; to abrogate	11.2
废止	fèizhǐ	to abolish	11.3
分寸	fēncun	proper limits for speech or action; sense of propriety	14.1
分割	fēngē	to cut apart; to break up	12.3
分化	fēnhuà	differentiation; polarization	15.3
坟墓	fénmù	grave; tomb	10.2
分外	fènwài	particularly; especially	13.2
奋斗	fèndòu	to strive; to struggle	15.4

风水宝地	fēngshuǐ bǎodì	place with auspicious geomantic omens	16.1
风水师	fēngshuǐshī	geomancer	16.1
风俗	fēngsú	custom; convention	9.1
风向	fēngxiàng	wind direction	16.1
佛像	fóxiàng	figure of Buddha	14.3
符号	fúhào	symbol; mark	9.4
辅助	fǔzhù	supplementary	15.2

G

生词	拼音	英文翻译	课序
改造	gǎizào	to transform; to reform	11.2
干预	gānyù	to intervene	14.2
感恩	gǎn'ēn	to feel grateful; to be thankful	10.1
感叹	gǎntàn	to sigh with feeling	15.3
高僧	gāosēng	eminent monk	14.3
高尚	gāoshàng	noble; lofty	11.1
戈壁	gēbì	gobi; the Gobi Desert	12.1
更迭	gēngdié	to change; to alternate	11.3
功名	gōngmíng	scholarly honour or official rank (in feudal times)	14.3
巩固	gǒnggù	to consolidate; to solidify	14.1
供奉	gòngfèng	to enshrine and worship	10.2

孤	gū	I; my (*used exclusively by the emperor in feudal China*)	10.4
顾名思义	gùmíng-sīyì	just as its name implies	13.3
寡人	guǎrén	I; my (*used exclusively by the emperor in feudal China*)	10.4
观念	guānniàn	concept; perception	10.1
观赏性	guānshǎngxìng	appreciation; enjoyability	15.3
官僚	guānliáo	bureaucrat	11.2
官职	guānzhí	official position	10.4
棺材	guāncai	coffin	10.2
管辖	guǎnxiá	to have jurisdiction over; to administer	11.4
广阔	guǎngkuò	vast; wide	12.2
归纳	guīnà	to conclude	15.1
龟甲	guījiǎ	tortoise shell	15.4
规矩	guīju	rule; custom	9.2
裹	guǒ	to wrap	13.2

H

生词	拼音	英文翻译	课序
海禁	hǎijìn	to ban on maritime trade or intercourse with foreign countries	12.2
豪华	háohuá	luxury	16.3
豪门	háomén	rich and powerful family	11.2
和美	héměi	harmonious and happy	16.3

和尚	héshang	monk	14.3
核心	héxīn	core	14.1
痕迹	hénjì	trace; trail	10.2
洪亮	hóngliàng	loud and clear; resonant	16.2
胡须	húxū	beard; moustache	16.4
糊涂	hútu	muddled	10.3
花轿	huājiào	bridal sedan chair	10.1
华侨	huáqiáo	overseas Chinese	9.1
环绕	huánrào	to embrace; to surround	16.2
缓慢	huǎnmàn	slow	15.3
换位	huànwèi	transposition	14.1
辉煌	huīhuáng	brilliant; splendid	12.2
回避	húibì	to avoid	10.5
回音	huíyīn	echo; aftersound	16.2
活力	huólì	vitality	15.2
火候	huǒhou	duration and degree of heating, cooking, smelting, etc.	9.1

J

生词	拼音	英文翻译	课序
吉利	jílì	lucky; auspicious	9.2
极致	jízhì	extreme	15.1

集会	jíhuì	assembly	13.1
集权	jíquán	centralization of state power	11.3
记载	jìzǎi	to record	11.1
忌讳	jìhuì	taboo	9.2
祭拜	jìbài	to worship	10.2
祭月	jìyuè	to offer oblations for the moon	13.3
寄托	jìtuō	to place (hope, etc.) on	13.3
假说	jiǎshuō	hypothesis	14.2
艰辛	jiānxīn	hardship	12.3
简化	jiǎnhuà	to simplify	9.4
鉴赏	jiànshǎng	to appreciate	9.4
僵化	jiānghuà	to become rigid; to ossify	11.2
降雨	jiàng yǔ	rainfall	16.4
脚印	jiǎoyìn	footprint	16.1
节奏	jiézòu	rhythm; cadence	15.3
解脱	jiětuō	to release	14.3
借鉴	jièjiàn	to use for reference	10.1
借助	jièzhù	to have the aid of	12.1
金碧辉煌	jīnbì-huīhuáng	splendid and magnificent	16.1
禁忌	jìnjì	taboo	10.3
经典	jīngdiǎn	classic	12.3
经络	jīngluò	main and collateral channels	15.2

经文	jīngwén	scriptures	12.1
精气	jīngqì	vital essence	15.2
敬称	jìngchēng	honorific title	10.4
敬酒	jìngjiǔ	to propose a toast	9.3
敬畏	jìngwèi	to hold in awe and veneration	16.2
鞠躬	jūgōng	to bow	10.1
巨著	jùzhù	monumental work; masterpiece	15.2
均匀	jūnyún	even; well-distributed	15.3
君主	jūnzhǔ	monarch; sovereign	14.1
郡县	jùnxiàn	the system of prefectures and counties	11.4

K

生词	拼音	英文翻译	课序
开幕式	kāimùshì	opening ceremony	16.1
开辟	kāipì	to open up	11.2
考核	kǎohé	to examine; to check	11.1
客房	kèfáng	guest room	16.3
口才	kǒucái	eloquence	14.1
叩头	kòutóu	to kowtow	10.2
宽容	kuānróng	lenient	15.4

L

生词	拼音	英文翻译	课序
礼	lǐ	the proprieties; etiquette	14.1
礼品	lǐpǐn	(complimentary) gift	9.4
历经	lìjīng	to go through	12.3
连襟	liánjīn	husbands of sisiters	10.3
鳞甲	línjiǎ	scale and shell (of fish or reptile)	16.4
灵感	línggǎn	inspiration	9.3
灵堂	língtáng	mourning hall	10.2
聆听	língtīng	to listen (respectfully)	16.4
流派	liúpài	school	14.2
琉璃瓦	liúliwǎ	glazed tile	16.2
聋	lóng	deaf	15.2
论辩	lùnbiàn	debate	14.1
绿洲	lǜzhōu	oasis	12.1

M

生词	拼音	英文翻译	课序
茅塞顿开	máosè-dùnkāi	to be enlightened all of a sudden	12.3
媒介	méijiè	medium	9.4
媒人	méiren	matchmaker	10.1
门当户对	méndāng-hùduì	well-matched marriage	10.1

门徒	méntú	disciple; follower	14.1
谜语	míyǔ	riddle	13.2
密度	mìdù	density	14.2
面壁	miànbì	to face the wall and meditate	15.3
面团	miàntuán	paste	13.3
渺小	miǎoxiǎo	minute; tiny	16.2
民居	mínjū	civil dwellings	16.3
名贵	míngguì	famous and precious	15.2
名目	míngmù	names of things; items	11.1
某	mǒu	some; certain	10.4

N

生词	拼音	英文翻译	课序
尼姑	nígū	Buddhist nun	14.3
酿造	niàngzào	to make (wine, vinegar, etc.); to brew (beer, etc.); to ferment	9.3
纽带	niǔdài	link; bond	10.3
农作物	nóngzuòwù	crops	16.4

O

生词	拼音	英文翻译	课序
偶尔	ǒu'ěr	occasionally	10.4

P

生词	拼音	英文翻译	课序
排列	páiliè	to line up	14.3
牌位	páiwèi	memorial tablet	10.2
庞大	pángdà	huge; enormous	11.2
陪葬	péizàng	to be buried with the dead	10.2
配套	pèitào	to match; to assort	11.3
喷吐	pēntǔ	to spurt	16.4
烹饪	pēngrèn	cooking	9.1
膨胀	péngzhàng	to expand	14.2
碰撞	pèngzhuàng	crash; collision	14.3
频繁	pínfán	often; frequently	12.2
品德	pǐndé	morality	11.1
平衡	pínghéng	balance	15.2
朴实	pǔshí	simple; plain	13.1
朴素	pǔsù	simple; plain	14.3
谱系	pǔxì	pedigree; ancestry	14.2

Q

生词	拼音	英文翻译	课序
其乐融融	qílè-róngróng	with happiness knowing no bounds	16.3

祈求	qíqiú	to pray	16.4
乞丐	qǐgài	beggar; pauper	9.2
启蒙	qǐméng	enlightenment	14.1
启示	qǐshì	enlightenment	15.4
起源	qǐyuán	origin	9.4
气氛	qìfēn	atmosphere	9.3
气功	qìgōng	a system of deep breathing exercises	15.3
气息	qìxī	breath	15.3
器官	qìguān	organ	15.2
器皿	qìmǐn	vessel	9.3
谦称	qiānchēng	modest title; self-abasing term	10.4
潜移默化	qiányí-mòhuà	to be unconsciously influenced	10.5
峭壁	qiàobì	cliff	14.3
惬意	qièyì	pleasant; cozy	16.3
青睐	qīnglài	favour; good graces	14.1
区划	qūhuà	division into districts	11.4

R

生词	拼音	英文翻译	课序
仁	rén	benevolence	14.1
认可	rènkě	to approve; to accept	11.2
任免	rènmiǎn	to appoint and remove	11.4

任用	rènyòng	to appoint; to give one a post	14.1
任人唯贤	rènrén-wéixián	to appoint people on their merits	11.1
融合	rónghé	to integrate	14.3
融入	róngrù	to blend in; to integrate	12.1
融为一体	róngwéiyìtǐ	integrated	16.2
柔和	róuhé	gentle; soft	15.3
儒家	Rújiā	Confucianist	14.1
入土为安	rùtǔ-wéi'ān	Burial brings peace to the deceased.	10.2
入座	rùzuò	to have a seat	9.2

S

生词	拼音	英文翻译	课序
丧葬	sāngzàng	burial; funeral	10.2
杀身之祸	shāshēnzhīhuò	fatal disaster	10.5
设置	shèzhì	to set up	13.2
神秘	shénmì	mysterious; mystical	14.2
神仙	shénxiān	immortal being	14.2
神谕	shényù	oracle	16.2
审美	shěnměi	appreciation of the beauty	14.2
肾脏	shènzàng	kidney	15.2
渗透	shèntòu	to permeate	15.1
圣地	shèngdì	holy land	12.3

圣上	shèngshàng	Your Majesty	10.4
盛行	shèngxíng	to prevail	12.3
使臣	shǐchén	envoy	12.2
士族	shìzú	(in feudal society) influential family of many generations	11.2
世家大族	shìjiā dàzú	aristocratic family	11.1
试图	shìtú	to attempt; to try	14.1
逝者	shìzhě	the dead	10.2
手段	shǒuduàn	means; method	11.1
首选	shǒuxuǎn	first choice	15.3
寿衣	shòuyī	graveclothes; shroud	10.2
兽骨	shòugǔ	animal bone	15.4
舒展	shūzhǎn	to stretch; to extend	15.3
衰落	shuāiluò	to decline	12.2
双向	shuāngxiàng	two-way; bothway	12.3
水源	shuǐyuán	source of water	16.1
顺畅	shùnchàng	unhindered; smooth	15.2
顺应	shùnyìng	to comply with; to conform to	14.2
说服	shuōfú	to persuade; to convince	14.1
四面八方	sìmiàn-bāfāng	all directions	16.2
俗话	súhuà	common saying; proverb	9.4
肃穆	sùmù	solemn and respectful	10.2
所谓	suǒwèi	so-called	12.3

T

生词	拼音	英文翻译	课序
太极	tàijí	*taiji*	15.1
太极拳	tàijíquán	*taijiquan*	15.3
探索	tànsuǒ	to explore	12.2
探望	tànwàng	to visit; to call on	10.2
特性	tèxìng	characteristic	16.4
提升	tíshēng	to promote; to improve	11.2
体系	tǐxì	system; setup	11.1
体现	tǐxiàn	to embody; to reflect	9.2
天伦之乐	tiānlúnzhīlè	happiness of a family	16.3
调节	tiáojié	to adjust	15.3
调整	tiáozhěng	to adjust	14.1
同心圆	tóngxīnyuán	concentric circles	16.2
统计	tǒngjì	statistics	9.4
透	tòu	with; through	13.2
凸	tū	bulge	15.1
图腾	túténg	totem	16.4
土质	tǔzhì	soil property	16.1
团圆	tuányuán	reunion	13.1
推移	tuīyí	to pass; to develop	11.2

W

生词	拼音	英文翻译	课序
晚辈	wǎnbèi	younger generation	16.3
万物	wànwù	all things on the earth	14.2
微臣	wēichén	humble servant	10.4
蔚为大观	wèiwéidàguān	to be indeed a splendid sight	12.1
吻合	wěnhé	to coincide	10.4
无处不在	wúchù-búzài	everywhere; anywhere	14.2
无坚不摧	wújiān-bùcuī	to be all-conquering	15.3
无可比拟	wúkěbǐnǐ	beyond comparison	12.2
五官	wǔguān	the five sense organs	15.2
五脏	wǔzàng	the five internal organs	15.2
武术	wǔshù	martial arts	15.3
务实	wùshí	to deal with concrete matters relating to work	14.3
误解	wùjiě	to misunderstand	9.3

X

生词	拼音	英文翻译	课序
吸引力	xīyǐnlì	attraction	14.2
稀少	xīshǎo	few; rare	12.2
习俗	xísú	custom	9.3

细节	xìjié	detail	10.3
细致	xìzhì	careful; meticulous	11.3
先人	xiānrén	ancestor; forefather	9.3
贤能	xiánnéng	able and virtuous personage	11.1
显然	xiǎnrán	obvious	13.2
馅儿	xiànr	filling; stuffing	13.2
相克	xiāngkè	restriction or checking relation in the Five Elements	15.1
相生	xiāngshēng	interpromoting relation in the Five Elements	15.1
香料	xiāngliào	perfume; spice	12.1
厢房	xiāngfáng	wing-room	16.3
向往	xiàngwǎng	to yearn for	12.1
削	xiāo	to cut	14.3
孝廉	xiàolián	filial and incorrupt	11.1
歇脚	xiējiǎo	to stop on the way for a rest	12.1
协调	xiétiáo	well-coordinated	16.1
辛勤	xīnqín	industrious; hard-working	13.1
行政	xíngzhèn	administration	11.4
修炼	xiūliàn	(of Taoists) to try to make pills of immortality and cultivate vital energy	14.2
虚构	xūgòu	imaginary	16.4
虚无	xūwú	nothingness; nihility	14.2
许愿	xǔyuàn	to make a wish	14.3

宣称	xuānchēng	to declare	16.2
选拔	xuǎnbá	to select	11.1
穴位	xuéwèi	acupoint	15.2
学派	xuépài	school of thought	14.1
血缘	xuèyuán	blood relationship; ties of blood	10.3
熏	xūn	to smoke; to fumigate	15.2

Y

生词	拼音	英文翻译	课序
延伸	yánshēn	to extend; to stretch	10.5
严峻	yánjùn	severe; austere	11.2
严密	yánmì	tight; close	11.3
沿用	yányòng	continue to use	11.4
演化	yǎnhuà	to evolute	14.2
演进	yǎnjìn	evolution	14.2
艳丽	yànlì	bright-colored and beautiful	13.1
宴请	yànqǐng	dinner; banquet	9.3
仰	yǎng	to face upward	13.2
药方	yàofāng	prescription	15.2
冶炼	yěliàn	to smelt	12.1
依次	yīcì	in sequence; one by one	9.2

意志	yìzhì	will; volition	14.2
因地取材	yīndì-qǔcái	to obtain raw materials locally	9.1
隐士	yǐnshì	hermit; recluse	14.3
印章	yìnzhāng	seal; stamp	15.1
迎娶	yíngqǔ	to marry (a woman)	10.1
用人	yòngren	servant	16.3
游学	yóuxué	to study in some other place or abroad	12.1
有缘	yǒuyuán	destined	13.2
寓意	yùyì	implied meaning	13.2
源源不断	yuányuán-búduàn	continuously	11.2
院落	yuànluò	courtyard	16.3
约束	yuēshù	constraint; restraint	14.1
运行	yùnxíng	to run; to operate	11.3
蕴含	yùnhán	to contain; to imply	14.2

Z

生词	拼音	英文翻译	课序
灾祸	zāihuò	disaster	16.2
造访	zàofǎng	to pay a visit; to call on	14.3
造就	zàojiù	to give rise to	14.2
栈道	zhàndào	plank road built along the face of a cliff	14.3

长辈	zhǎngbèi	elder; senior	16.3
哲学	zhéxué	philosophy	14.2
针灸	zhēnjiǔ	acupuncture	15.2
真相	zhēnxiàng	truth	12.3
朕	zhèn	I; my (*used exclusively by the emperor in feudal China*)	10.4
蒸馏	zhēngliú	to distill	9.3
正月	zhēngyuè	the first lunar month	13.2
正房	zhèngfáng	principal room (in a courtyard, usually facing south)	16.3
正式	zhèngshì	formal	9.3
正统	zhèngtǒng	orthodox	14.1
肢体	zhītǐ	limbs and trunk	15.3
职位	zhíwèi	occupation	9.2
至高无上	zhìgāo-wúshàng	supreme	10.4
中央	zhōngyāng	the highest leading body of state power	11.3
中庸	zhōngyǒng	golden mean; moderation	14.1
中轴线	zhōngzhóuxiàn	central axis	16.1
周游	zhōuyóu	to travel round	14.1
妯娌	zhóuli	wives of brothers	10.3
主张	zhǔzhāng	proposal; opinion	14.1
炷	zhù	*a measure word for incense*	10.2
爪子	zhuǎzi	talon	16.4

庄稼	zhuāngjia	crops	13.3
庄严	zhuāngyán	solemn; dignified	10.2
装点	zhuāngdiǎn	to decorate	13.2
追溯	zhuīsù	trace back to	9.4
资源	zīyuán	resource	10.2
总结	zǒngjié	to sum up; to summarize	11.3
纵线	zòngxiàn	ordinate	16.1
祖籍	zǔjí	ancestral home	9.1
遵守	zūnshǒu	to follow; to abide by	10.5
坐标	zuòbiāo	coordinate	10.3
坐牢	zuòláo	to be imprisoned; to be in jail	10.5

附录03

练习参考答案

Reference Answers to the Exercises

第九课

9.1

1. D
2. ABCE
3. D
4. A—煮；B—煎；C—蒸；D—炒；E—烤；F—炸。
5. 略

9.2

1. D
2. ACD
3. D
4. 略

9.3

1. D
2. ABC
3. D
4. 略

9.4

1. √×√ ×××
2. B
3. 绿茶—不发酵—杭州龙井；红茶—完全发酵—祁门红茶；乌龙茶—半发酵—安溪铁观音；花茶—绿茶或红茶中加入香花—茉莉花茶。
4. B
5. 略

第十课

10.1

1. D
2. C
3. A
4. A—羌族；B—汉族；C—壮族；D—阿昌族。

10.2

1. B
2. B
3. A
4. 略

10.3

1. AD
2. B
3. 爸爸的哥哥—伯伯；妈妈的兄弟—舅舅；丈夫对外人称呼妻子的父母—岳父、岳母；父母对外人称呼女儿的丈夫—女婿、姑爷；古时候丈夫对外称呼自己的妻子—贱内、拙荆；两个姐妹各自丈夫之间的关系—连襟。

10.4

1. C
2. C
3. A
4. 略

10.5

1. ××√×√√√
2. C
3. C
4. 略

第十一课

11.1

1.A
2.D
3.C
4.略

11.2

1. D
2. D
3. A
4. 略

11.3

1. C
2. C
3. B
4. C

11.4

1.√×√√×√
2. B
3. C

第十二课

12.1

1. ABCD
2. D
3. C
4. D

12.2

1. B
2. B
3. C
4. D

12.3

1. ×√√√×√
2. C
3. D
4. ACD

第十三课

13.1

1. D
2. C
3. B
4. AD
5. 略

13.2

1. AC
2. D
3. 1）橘子；2）花生；3）兔子；4）荷花。

13.3

1. ×√√√×√
2. C
3. ABC
4.略

第十四课

14.1

1. D
2. C
3. D
4. ABCD
5. 略

14.2

1. B
2. C
3. D
4. CD

5. 儒家思想—克己复礼为仁；仁者见仁，智者见智；非礼勿视，非礼勿听。道家思想—道可道，非常道；天地之道，极则反，盈则损。

14.3

1. ×√×√√×√
2. D
3. AB
4. B
5. 削去头发做和尚的人—佛教；
求取功名的读书人—儒家思想；
回归乡野，过着宁静朴素的生活的人—道家思想。

第十五课

15.1

1. ABC
2. B
3. C
4. ABC

15.2

1. C
2. ABCD
3. C
4. C
5. CD

15.3

1. D
2. A
3. ACD
4. D

15.4

1. √××√×√
2. C
3. B
4. ABCD

第十六课

16.1

1. C
2. BCD
3. D
4. 略

16.2

1. D
2. B
3. B
4. ABC

16.3

1. B
2. C
3. D
4. B

16.4

1. ×√√×√√√
2. D
3. D
4. ABCDE
5. 略